SUPERCOOL
SCIENCE
EXPERIMENTS

ARCTURUS

ARCTURUS

This edition published in 2015 by Arcturus Publishing Limited
26/27 Bickels Yard, 151–153 Bermondsey Street,
London SE1 3HA

Photography by Sally Henry, Trevor Cook and Shutterstock except for
p6-7 Javier Trueba/MSF/Science Photo Library; p42-43 Ocean/Corbis;
p62-63, p76-77, p102-103, p210-211, and p252-253 NASA;
p86-87 Wikipedia Commons; p112-113 Science Photo Library
(Steve Gschmeissner); and 142-143 Photo Researchers/FLPA.
3-D images on p90-91 by Pinsharp 3D Graphics
Illustrations by Andrew Painter
Design by Notion Design

ISBN: 978-1-78404-813-6
CH004567US

Supplier 29, Date 0715, Print run 4208

Printed in China

Introduction

This book is jam-packed full of supercool science experiments for you to amaze your family and friends with. Some of the experiments are really simple, while others are a little bit tricky and may need more equipment or the help of an adult.

Every experiment includes a list of all the equipment you'll need to do it. We've made sure all of these items are easy to get hold of, so you can get started with the fun part—doing the experiment.

We've also added a scientific explanation of each experiment in the panel "How does it work?" That way, you can astound your friends and family with your incredible scientific knowledge.

Have fun!

Contents

Material World   6

Lava Lamp   8
Mint Volcano   11
Balloon Kebab   14
Magnetic Cereal   16
Fossil Focus   18
Bubble Bomb   20
Gloopy Goop   22
Coin Cleaner   24
Crystal Creations   26
Cabbage Detector   28
Oil and Water   30
Color Storm   32
Secret Colors   34
Invisible Ink   36
Dense and Denser   38
Does Air Weigh Anything?   40

Bright Ideas   76

Kaleidoscope   78
Hall of Mirrors   81
A Box Full of Sky   84
Amazing Aurora   86
3-D Glasses   88
Trick Your Eyes!   92
Light Top   94
Make Your Own Zoetrope   97
Rainbow Maker   100
Night Lights   102
Pepper's Ghost   104
Light Trap   106
Color Mix-Up   108
Seeing Around Corners   110

Push and Pull   42

Book Battle   44
Weird Water   46
Marble Madness   48
Balancing Butterfly   50
Under Pressure   52
Homemade Compass   54
Wobbler Toy   56
Parachute Jump   59
Spacewalk   62
Down to Earth   64
Jet Propulsion   66
Sink or Swim?   68
Thread Reel Racer   70
Air Force   72
Balloon Fun   74

Super Sonic   112

Make Your Own Drum Set   114
Paper Popper   117
Dancing Flame   120
What a Noise!   122
Funky Bone Vibrations   124
Where's That Sound?   126
Paper Kazoo   128
Cup Screech   130
Whale Song   132
Secret Sounds   134
Seeing Sound   136
In Tune?   138
Bouncing Sound   140

It's Alive 142

Growing Seeds 144
Which Way Is Up? 146
Silly Celery 148
The Perfect Place for Plants 150
Stone Flowers 152
House for a Louse 154
A Wormery 156
Bug Hunters 158
Spotted! 160
Yeast Balloon 162
Bottle Bird Feeder 164
Pine Cones 165
DNA From Strawberries 167
Ready for My Close-Up 170
Bending a Chicken Bone 172
How Big Are Your Lungs? 174
Seeing Things 176
Mystery Box 178

Hot Stuff 180

Hot Topic: Conduction 182
Moving Story: Convection 184
Warming Glow: Radiation 186
Blubber Glove 188
Fire Show 190
The Water Cycle 192
Bigger & Hotter: Expansion 194
Mighty Ice 196
Antifreeze 198
Ice Cube Trick 199
Ice Castles 200
Disappearing Act 202
Mini Melt 204
Homemade Shrink Ray 207
Sun Burst 210
Solar Still 212
Feeling Hot and Cold 214
Ice Cream in a Bag 216
Solar Oven 219
Soap Sculptures 222
Jumping Coin 224
Balloon Flame 226
Jar Wars 228

Super Power 230

Making a Circuit 232
Go with the Flow 234
Turn It On! 236
Bright Ideas 238
Lightning Strikes! 240
The Lemon Battery 242
This Page Is Alarmed! 244
Attractive Stuff 246
Magnetic Games 248
The Magnetic Earth 250
Mighty Magnets 252

Glossary 254

5

MATERIAL WORLD

Everything around you is made of matter. In fact, everything inside you is, too! In this chapter, you'll find facts and experiments that explore the incredible science of materials.

Thousands of years ago, water containing a mineral named gypsum filtered slowly through these caves, forming the enormous pillars you can see in this photograph.

Lava Lamp

Lava lamps are cool decorations that are fascinating to look at. They are also surprisingly simple to make.

You will need

- A clean plastic bottle or jar
- A funnel
- Vegetable oil
- Food coloring
- Effervescent vitamin tablet
- A flashlight
- Water

Step 1

Fill a bottle or jar ¼ full with water. Add 10 drops of food coloring.

Step 2

Fill the bottle to the top with vegetable oil.

Step 3

Break the vitamin tablet into four small pieces.

Step 4

Drop one piece of the vitamin tablet into the bottle. Watch the result!

Step 5

To improve the lava lamp effect, turn off the lights, turn on the flashlight, and shine it through the bottle.

Experiment with different jars and bottles and other food colorings. Which work the best?

How does it work?

Oil and water do not mix. When you add oil to water, it usually just sits on its own in a separate layer on top of the water. However, adding the piece of tablet to the container changes this. The tablet reacts with the water, creating bubbles of carbon dioxide gas that rise to the surface. The oil and water are stirred up by the bubbles.

Mint Volcano

Get ready for an edible eruption! In this experiment, you'll discover that mixing chewy mints and diet cola can have explosive results.

You will need

- Two packages of strawberry-flavored jello
- A pack of chewy mints
- Hot water
- A large mixing bowl
- A small glass
- A can of diet cola
- A plate
- A tray

Step 1

Take two packages of jello. Follow the instructions on the package to make a jello mixture.

WARNING!
Ask an adult to help you with the hot water.

Step 2

Take a big bowl. Turn a glass upside down inside it.

Step 3

Pour the jello mixture into the bowl. Make sure it covers the glass.

Step 4

Put the jello in the refrigerator to set. When the jello has set, turn it out onto a flat plate and remove the glass.

Step 5

Put the plate onto a tray. Take the jello outside, then pour diet cola into the cavity left by the glass.

Step 6

Drop six chewy mints into the cola. Watch out—it will erupt!

How does it work?

The bubbles in a cola drink are made up of carbon dioxide gas. They have been forced into the drink under pressure. When you drop a chewy mint into the cola, the carbon dioxide bubbles collect together and grow in the tiny dents on the surface of the mint. Then the bubbles rush out in a big eruption.

Balloon Kebab

If someone told you they could stick a sharp object through a balloon without popping it, you wouldn't believe them would you? But it is possible. Amaze your family and friends by making a genuine balloon kebab.

You will need

- Balloons
- A wooden kebab skewer
- Vegetable oil

Step 1

Blow up a balloon to about half its full size, and tie a knot in the neck.

Step 2

Hold the balloon in one hand and the kebab skewer in the other.

Step 3

Poke the point of the skewer into the balloon, near the knot. Wipe a little vegetable oil on the skewer, so that the skewer slides in smoothly.

Step 4

Push the skewer through the balloon very gently, twisting as you push. Aim to make it come out on the opposite side, at the middle of the top of the balloon.

Step 5

If you have a long skewer or small balloons, try to add more balloons—like a kebab!

If you poke the balloon in the middle with the skewer, it will pop!

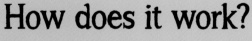

How does it work?

Usually, when a balloon is stabbed with a kebab skewer, the rubber skin will tear and it will pop. That is because the pressurized air inside the balloon is stretching the skin very tight, so that the slightest hole blows open in an instant. However, the skin is not as tight at the "ends" of a balloon. So stabbing it there won't pop it—as long as you're careful.

15

Magnetic Cereal

Is the iron contained in food the same thing as the metal iron? Try this experiment to find out.

You will need

- Cereal fortified with iron (look at the small print on the box)
- A rolling pin
- A small plastic bag
- A very strong magnet—a "rare earth" magnet will work well
- A cereal bowl
- Water

The bag keeps the cereal together.

Step 1

Crush some cereal into a fine powder in a small bag.

Step 2

Put the magnet in the powder and roll it around.

16

Try shaking the powder off—the magnetic attraction won't let you!

Step 3

Take the magnet out of the bag. It should have crumbs of cereal sticking to it.

Step 4

Take a clean cereal bowl and fill it almost to the top with water.

Step 5

When the water has stopped any movement, drop a large flake of cereal on the surface, in the middle of the bowl.

Step 6

By holding your magnet just above the cereal flake, you should be able to draw it across the surface of the water without touching it!

How does it work?

This experiment shows that fortified cereals, like many other foods, contain iron in small amounts. It is very important that you get enough iron in your diet. Iron helps your blood to carry oxygen around the body. If you don't have enough of it, you may feel tired and unwell.

Fossil Focus

When an animal or plant dies, it usually decays quickly. But sometimes an animal's body sinks into deep mud and lies there, undisturbed, for millions of years. As time passes, the mud presses down on the remains. Minerals dissolved in the mud turn the remains to stone. These remains are called fossils. Fossils give us clues about what life was like on Earth millions of years ago. Without fossils, we wouldn't know about dinosaurs or prehistoric sea creatures like this one.

Bubble Bomb

This fun and safe "bomb" will explode with a loud pop!

You will need

- Water
- A measuring cup
- A plastic ziplock bag
- A paper towel
- 2 tablespoons of baking soda
- Vinegar

Step 1

Find a place where making a mess won't be terrible—outside, or maybe in the bathtub if the weather's bad.

Step 2

Test your bag for leaks. Put water in it, close the seal, and turn it upside down. If no water leaks out, it's OK to use.

Step 3

Tear a piece of paper towel, about 5 inches (15 cm) square. Put 2 tablespoons of baking soda in the center of the square and fold the paper around it.

Step 4

Mix 10 fluid ounces (300 ml) of vinegar with 5 fluid ounces (150 ml) of warm water, then pour them into the plastic bag.

Step 5

Put the paper towel package into the bag. Hold it in the corner away from the vinegar while you seal the bag.

Step 6

Place the bag on the floor—and stand back! The bag will swell up ...

Step 7

... and then pop!

How does it work?

Vinegar is an acid and baking soda is a base. When you mix acids and bases together, they react and turn into different chemicals. When carbon dioxide gas forms in our experiment, there isn't enough room for it in the plastic bag. So the pressure builds up, and the bag swells and pops, releasing the gas.

21

Gloopy Goop

This strange slime is not really a liquid but not really a solid, either! Make some for yourself to find out what kind of material it is.

You will need

- 1 cup of cornflour
- ½ cup of water
- A mixing bowl
- Food coloring

Step 1

Pour a cup of cornflour into a mixing bowl. It should feel smooth and silky in your hands.

Step 2

Add two drops of food coloring to the water. You really don't need very much!

Step 3

Mix the water into the flour, using your fingers. How does the mixture feel now?

Step 4

Try squeezing a handful of the liquid you've made into a ball. It will become a solid!

Step 5

Let the goop settle into the bottom of the bowl. Touch the surface gently, then tap it hard.

Step 6

If you hold your hand still, it will become liquid and run through your fingers.

How does it work?

When this mixture is put under pressure, the cornflour molecules are forced together and it behaves like a solid. When it is handled gently, the cornflour molecules can move around freely, and it flows like a liquid. Quicksand works in just the same way!

Coin Cleaner

Many people like to collect coins from different countries. However, coins tarnish easily and can soon start to look dirty. Here is how you can give them back their shine.

You will need

- Dirty coins
- Cola
- A plastic cup
- A paper towel
- An old toothbrush

Step 1

Take some dirty coins. Why not take a photograph to compare results later on?

Step 2

Rinse a coin in water to remove any loose dirt.

Step 3

Put the coin in a plastic cup, then pour in some cola.

Step 4

After 20 minutes, take the coin out and dry it.

Step 5

Repeat the process until the coin is clean. With a really dirty coin, it may help to scrub the cola on the coin using an old toothbrush.

Step 6

Take photos of your coin at intervals to see the rate of change. Here's a very dirty old coin, with results after 30 minutes, 2 hours, 6 hours, 12 hours, and a day.

How does it work?

Cola drinks are more acidic than you might think! The cola wears down the top layer of the coins. That makes them look sparkly and clean.

Crystal Creations

A crystal is a solid material that forms itself into a very regular 3-D pattern. Crystals form when liquid cools, hardens, and turns into a solid. The arrangement of atoms in the solid produces the shape of the crystal. An example of this is when water is cooled and becomes ice.

Experiment 1

You will need

- Coarse string
- An ice pop stick
- Hot water
- A spoon
- Salt, sand, soil, sugar
- 2 glass jars
- A plastic bag
- Coffee filter paper or paper towel
- A funnel
- A small plate

Step 1

Put some hot water into a glass jar. Water from the hot faucet should be hot enough.

Step 2

Add sugar, one spoon at a time, using the ice pop stick to stir. Keep adding more sugar until you can't dissolve any more. You'll see undissolved sugar left at the bottom of the jar.

water level

end of string

Step 3

Tie the string to the ice pop stick, hang it in the sugar solution, and leave to cool. The string is a good surface for growing crystals.

Step 4

As the solution cools, crystals begin to form on the string. Be patient: It can take a few days for crystals to form, provided you have made a saturated solution.

How does it work?

The sugar dissolves in water to form a sugar solution. Hot water allows more sugar to dissolve. As the water cools, it cannot hold as much sugar in solution, and some sugar changes back to a solid.

Experiment 2

Step 1

Mix salt, soil, and sand together thoroughly with a spoon, on a piece of plastic bag.

Step 2

Stir the mixture into warm water. Leave it to settle overnight.

Step 3

Place the filter paper in a funnel, then pour the liquid through, being careful to leave the sediment in the bottom of the jar. Leave the filtered liquid on the plate in a warm place.

How does it work?

Only the salt dissolves in the water. The heavier particles of sand and soil sink to the bottom of the jar. Filtering removes the smaller sand and soil particles. Finally, on the plate, the water *evaporates* to leave just the salt crystals.

Cabbage Detector

You can use cabbage water to test whether liquids are acids, *neutral*, or *alkaline*. Examples of acids are acetic acid (in vinegar) and citric acid (in oranges and lemons).

You will need

- **Knife for chopping**
- **2 glasses**
- **Heat-resistant bowls or jars**
- **White vinegar**
- **Baking soda**
- **Plastic dropper**
- **Boiling water**
- **Red cabbage**

Step 1

Ask an adult to chop about two cupfuls of cabbage into small pieces. Place them in the bowl.

WARNING!
Ask an adult to help you with the hot water.

Step 2

Ask an adult to pour some boiling water into a bowl of red cabbage, then leave it for 15 minutes.

Step 3

Pour off the liquid into a bowl. This liquid is our "indicator."

Step 4

You need two known liquids to test your indicator. We are using white vinegar (acid) and a solution of baking soda in water (alkaline).

Step 5

Add indicator to your solution in drops. Watch the indicator color change. Wash the glasses thoroughly between tests.

Step 6

See where the results fall on this chart.

◄ more acidic neutral more alkaline ►

red purple blue-violet blue-green green-yellow

Try other kinds of colored vegetable juice to see if they make indicators.

How does it work?

The pigments or colors from the cabbage react with acids and alkalis to change the color. The juice should turn pink in acidic solutions and green in alkaline ones. Put some indicator drops in plain water. This is your neutral color. Use your indicator to test other liquids and compare the results.

Oil and Water

Some things don't get along well together. Take oil and water. These two can never be good friends, no matter how hard you try to mix or shake them together. If an oil tanker loses its oil at sea, a thick layer of crude oil sits on the surface of the water, causing problems for birds and fish. Oil from cars forms a greasy film on the top of puddles in the street. Even in a salad, the oil separates from the rest of the dressing. The scientific word for this is immiscible.

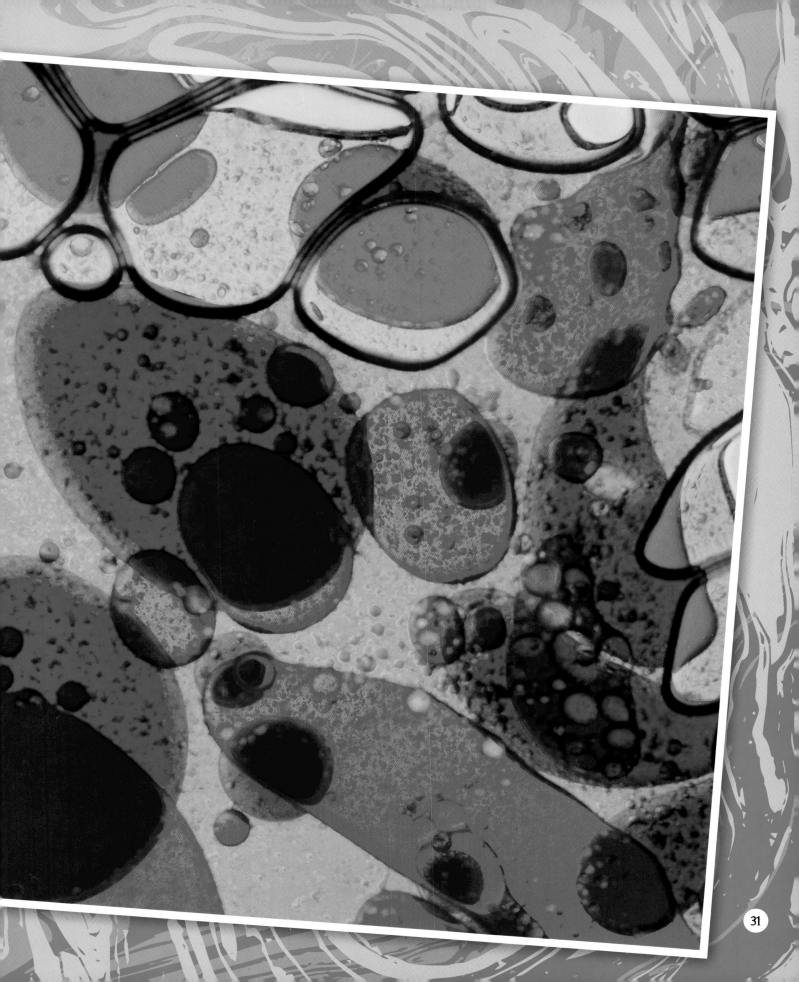

Color Storm

Oil and water don't mix. Or do they? In fact, milk contains both. Here's how you use oil and water to make a supercool pattern.

You will need

- 2 white plates
- Whole milk
- Dishwashing liquid
- A matchstick or skewer
- 3 or 4 colors of food coloring
- A notebook and pencil

Step 1

Pour water into a white plate. Wait for a minute or until the water stops moving.

Step 2

Put some evenly spaced drops of food coloring in the water.

Step 3

Pour some milk into the other plate. Wait for a minute for the milk to stop moving.

Step 4

Put some drops of food coloring in the milk, evenly spaced.

32

Step 5

Add one drop of dishwashing liquid to each of the plates.

Step 6

Look at your plates after a few minutes, then again after 10 minutes.

Step 7

Look at your plates again after 20 minutes. Use a notebook and pencil to write down the results.

Make notes of what you see:

- What happens when you add the food coloring to the water?

- What happens when you add the coloring to the milk?

- What happens when you add the dishwashing liquid to the water and milk?

- Keep reading to find out why ...

How does it work?

Milk is a special mixture of fat and water called an emulsion. The fat is not dissolved in the water, but the two are mixed together. (Cream at the top of milk is some of the fat that has separated.)

The food coloring doesn't travel through milk as easily as it does through water because it mixes with only the watery part of the milk.

When you add dishwashing liquid, two things happen. First, the surface tension of the water is destroyed. Then, the fat and water start to mix together because the dishwashing liquid breaks up the fat.

The movement of the food coloring shows you what's happening. It moves to the side of the saucer when the surface tension is broken, and it swirls in patterns as the fat and water start to mix together.

Secret Colors

Chromatography is a way of separating the parts that make up a mixture. We are going to use one type of chromatography, called paper chromatography, to find out what pigments make up different colored inks.

You will need

- Colored felt-tip pens (not permanent or waterproof)
- Blotting paper
- A ruler
- Scissors
- Tape
- Bowl
- Water
- Pencil
- Notebook

Step 1

Cut blotting paper into six strips, 6 x ½ in (100 x 15 mm).

Step 2

Number the strips and tape them to the ruler.

Step 3

Put a small dot of a different color on each strip, noting each strip number as the color is put on.

Step 4

Fill the bowl half full with water. Hang the strips over the edge of the bowl, so that the ends are just touching the water.

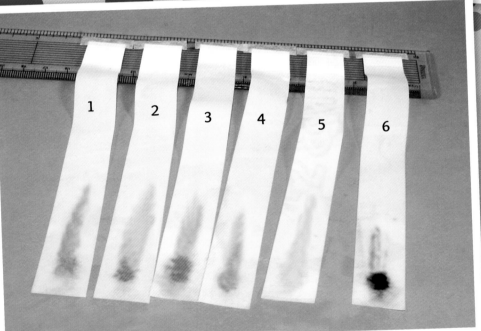

Step 5

Wait until the water is ¾ inch (20 mm) or so from the ruler, then remove the strips from the bowl, and record the colors you see. Sometimes a black will give a very surprising result!

How does it work?

Water moves up the strips by capillary action and carries the pigments with it. Some pigments are more strongly attracted to the paper fibers and so are not carried so far. A color may be made of many different pigments.

Invisible Ink

It's easy to send secret messages when you write them in top secret invisible ink! This is a supercool experiment to try with friends. The "secret" lies in the combination of lemon juice and heat from a light bulb or an iron. Let's try drawing a treasure map first!

You will need

- A toothpick
- A lemon
- A small knife
- Paper
- A bowl
- Heat source, such as a light bulb or iron

Step 1

Ask an adult to cut a lemon in half for you. Squeeze the lemon juice into a small bowl.

Step 2

The lemon juice is your "ink"! Dip the round end of a toothpick into the bowl.

WARNING!
Ask an adult to help you cut the lemon in half.

Step 3

Draw a secret map on some paper. Use lots of lemon juice for each part of the map you draw.

Step 4

Allow the paper to dry until you can't see the drawing anymore!

Step 5

Now move the paper back and forth under a heat source. As the lemon juice "ink" gets warm, your secret map is revealed.

How does it work?

The acid in the lemon juice breaks down the cellulose of the paper into sugars. The heat source tends to caramelize the sugars, making them brown and revealing your secret drawing.

Dense and Denser

If you take two similar-size cubes of wood and lead, the one made of lead would be much heavier. This is because lead is more dense than wood. It has more material packed into the same space.

You will need

- Glass jar
- 3 drinking glasses
- Various liquids: syrup, cooking oil, water
- Various solids: grape, coin, plastic wine cork
- Blue and red food coloring
- Plastic dropper

Experiment 1

Step 1

Gently pour the cooking oil, syrup, and water into a glass, one at a time.

cooking oil

water

syrup

Step 2

Let the liquids settle. They should form distinct layers.

38

Step 3

We are going to put the grape, the coin, and the cork into the jar. Where do you think they will settle?

grape in water on top of syrup

coin sinks to base of syrup

cork floats in oil

How does it work?

The various substances float or sink according to their densities.

Experiment 2

Step 1

Take a small glass of cold water and add some drops of blue food coloring. Put it in the refrigerator for an hour or so.

Step 2

Take a small glass of hot water (from the faucet) and add some red food coloring.

Step 3

Half fill a tall glass with the blue water from the refrigerator.

Step 4

Use the dropper to transfer small amounts of the red water into the blue water. The idea is not to mix the two colors. Keep the end of the plastic dropper near the surface.

How does it work?

If you have managed to do this experiment carefully enough, there should be two distinct layers. What do you think the position of the layers tells us about their density? Warm water is less dense than cold water. For this reason, the red-colored water stays above the blue water in the drinking glass.

Does Air Weigh Anything?

Air doesn't weigh anything ... or does it? Let's find out with this really fun and easy experiment!

You will need

- 2 balloons
- String
- Scissors
- Thin piece of wood, about 2 feet (60 cm) long
- Balloons
- A marker pen

Step 1

Make marks about ¾ inch (1 cm) from each end of the piece of wood.

Step 2

Suspend the wood by a piece of string, so that it hangs horizontally. This is our weighing *scale*.

Step 3

Ask an adult to help you cut two pieces of string the same length—about 6 inches (15 cm). Make a loop at the end of each piece, just big enough to slip over the wood.

Step 4

Take two similar balloons. Blow them both up, tie off the neck of one, but let the air out of the other.

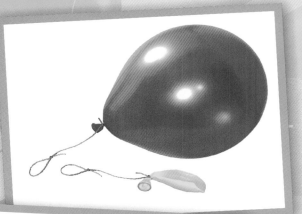

Step 5

Tie each balloon to one of the strings.

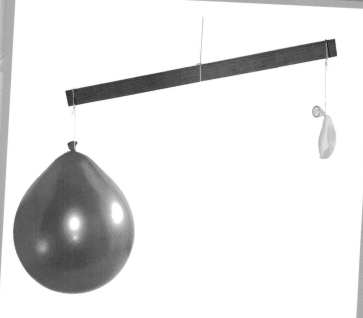

Step 6

Slip the strings onto the stick, exactly on the ½ inch (12 mm) marks.

How does it work?

The only difference between the two balloons is that one is "empty," and the other is full of air. But the air in the balloon is slightly compressed, so it is denser than the air around it, making the scale tip down.

41

PUSH AND PULL

In this chapter, we explore the science of forces. Forces are all around us and are acting on us all the time!

This man is skysurfing high above the Earth! This is made possible by the forces of gravity (pulling him down) and air resistance (slowing his fall).

Book Battle

This fantastic trick might seem like fiction, but actually it's all about friction!

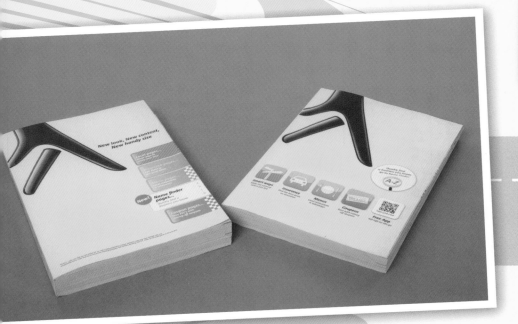

Step 1

Take two big, thick books, with plenty of pages.

Step 2

Turn a page from each book alternately, so that they overlap by an inch or two.

44

Step 3

Continue until the books are completely combined.

Step 4

Find two volunteers, and ask them whether they think they can pull the books apart. It looks easy—but in fact, it is impossible!

How does it work?

When you slide two pages across each other, a force called friction resists the movement. When all the pages of a book are overlapped as in our experiment, that friction is multiplied by the number of pages. That's a lot of friction—so it's actually impossible for anyone to pull the books apart!

45

Weird Water

This fiendishly clever bit of science can be used as a perfect practical joke to play on your friends and family!

You will need

- A plastic water bottle
- Water
- A thumbtack
- An outdoor space—this could get messy!

Step 1

Fill a plastic water bottle all the way up to the top.

Step 2

Screw the cap on firmly.

46

Step 3

Make holes around the sides of the bottle with a thumbtack. The water won't come out—yet! Now take your bottle somewhere that you don't mind getting wet.

Step 4

Ask a friend if they would like a drink of water, and hand them the bottle.

Step 5

When they open the lid ... the water will pour out of the holes. They're going to get soaked!

Try doing the same experiment with a soft-sided container, like a large plastic bag. Fill the bag with water, hold it up with one hand, and make holes with the thumbtack.

How does it work?

Water cannot escape through the holes while the lid is on, because the air pressure pushing on the side of the bottle is stronger than the downward pull of gravity on the water. But when the lid is removed, air rushes in and adds its force to gravity's pull ... and SPLASH!

Marble Madness

This experiment can be performed as a magic trick. Tell your family and friends that you are going to pick up a marble in a glass without touching the marble.

You will need

- A wine glass
- A marble
- A lot of patience and practice
- An audience to show the trick to!

Step 1

You will need a wine glass shaped like this.

This part is the bowl. It needs to be wider in the middle than at the rim.

Step 2

Ask a volunteer if they can pick up a marble without touching it or using the glass to scoop it up. They won't be able to!

Step 3

Now show them how it's done. Place the glass over the marble. Hold the glass by the base, and start gently moving it in a circular motion.

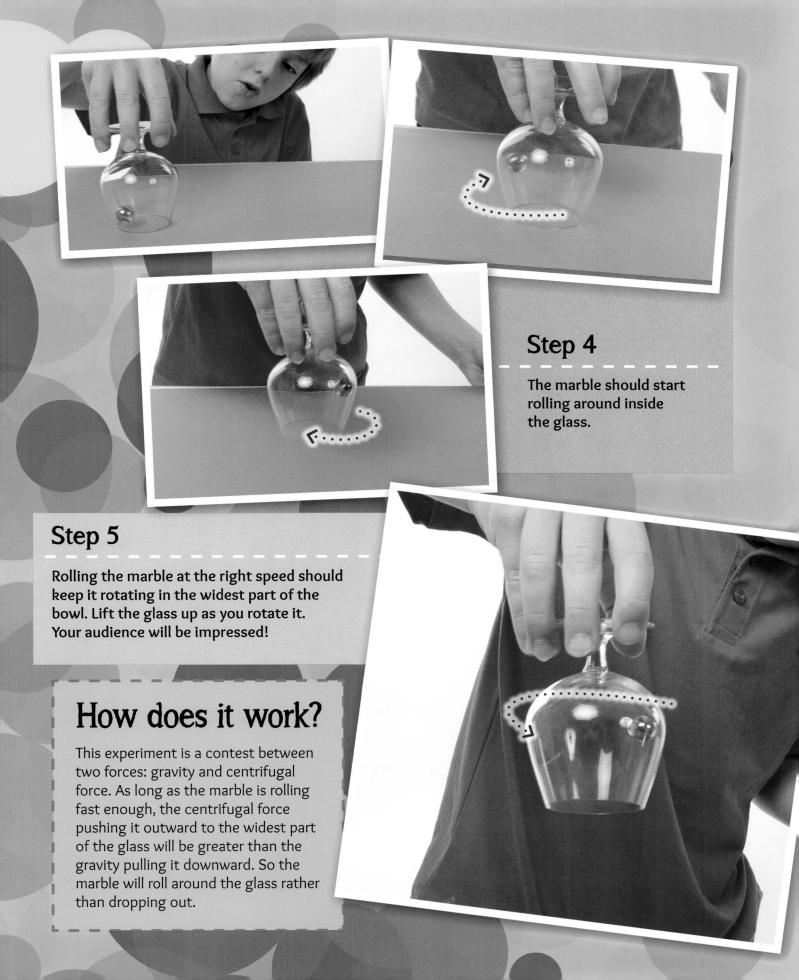

Step 4

The marble should start rolling around inside the glass.

Step 5

Rolling the marble at the right speed should keep it rotating in the widest part of the bowl. Lift the glass up as you rotate it. Your audience will be impressed!

How does it work?

This experiment is a contest between two forces: gravity and centrifugal force. As long as the marble is rolling fast enough, the centrifugal force pushing it outward to the widest part of the glass will be greater than the gravity pulling it downward. So the marble will roll around the glass rather than dropping out.

Balancing Butterfly

Is it possible to balance a piece of paper on a single finger? Sure it is! Here's how to make a beautiful, balancing butterfly.

Step 1

Draw a butterfly shape on a piece of thin cardstock. The tips of the wings must be above the head.

Step 2

Ink over the lines with a black marker. Decorate the body and wings with colored pens or paints.

Step 3

Cut out the shape with scissors.

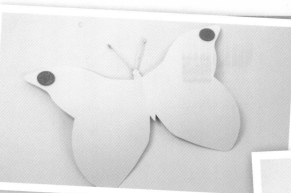

Step 4

Glue matching coins to the tips of the wings.

Step 5

Bend the wings down a little.

Step 6

You should be able to balance the butterfly on the tip of your finger! The balance point should be near the head, depending on the weight of your coins and the cardstock thickness.

Step 7

You can put butterflies all around the room, on furniture, mirrors, ornaments, flowerpots— wherever there's a place for them to balance!

How does it work?

When the coin weights are added to the butterfly, the center of gravity falls almost directly between them, which is where your finger is, so it makes it easy to balance.

Under Pressure

The air around you has weight, and it presses down on everything it touches. That pressure is called atmospheric pressure. It is the force that is exerted on a surface by the air above it as gravity pulls it to Earth. However, water is much denser than air. A column of water that is 33 feet (10 meters) thick exerts the same pressure on a person as the entire Earth's atmosphere! Divers are careful not to descend too far, too quickly, since the pressure can be dangerous.

Homemade Compass

You will never be lost again once you know how to make your own compass!

You will need

- **A glass**
- **Water**
- **A sewing needle (be careful of the point!)**
- **Thin cardstock**
- **Scissors**
- **A pencil**
- **Colored markers**
- **A bar magnet**

Step 1

Hold a needle in one hand, then stroke the north end of a magnet along its length 50 times, from point to eye.

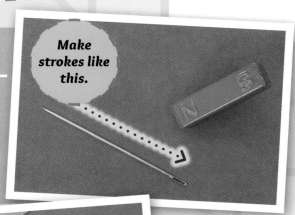

Make strokes like this.

Step 2

Using scissors, cut a piece of thin cardstock in an arrow shape, just a little longer than your needle.

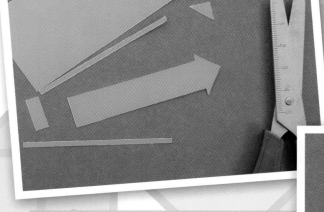

Step 3

Thread the needle through the cardstock, making sure the point is at the same end as the arrow.

Step 4

Fill a glass with water.

Step 5

Gently lower the arrow onto the water.

Step 6

The arrow should point toward the north!

Step 7

Now that you know which direction is north, write all the other compass points on a piece of cardstock that is a little larger than your glass.

Place your glass on top of the cardstock.

How does it work?

When you rub the needle with the magnet, it becomes a weak magnet itself and will automatically point to the magnetic North Pole. By floating it on the water, you reduce the friction. This allows the needle to easily turn around and point in the direction it is attracted to.

Wobbler Toy

This wobbler toy makes a great gift! No matter how much it wobbles, it will never fall down.

You will need

- A table tennis ball
- Scissors
- A piece of paper
- A ruler
- A pencil
- Colored markers
- Tape
- Modeling clay
- A glue stick

Step 1

Get an adult to help you cut a table tennis ball in half, using scissors.

Step 2

Cut out a rectangle of paper measuring 5 x 2 inches (13 x 5 cm). Draw a line about half an inch (1 cm) from one narrow end.

Draw your figure in the center of the paper.

Step 3

Draw a face and body on the paper, like this. We're going to decorate this one as a fairy, but there are other ideas on page 58.

Step 4

Roll the paper into a tube, overlapping as far as the pencil line. Fix it in place with the glue stick.

Step 5

Tape one half of the ball to each end. Finish drawing the top of the head.

Step 6

She won't stand up yet!

Step 7

Take the foot end off. Put a lump of modeling clay in the middle of the half ball, and stick it back on the body.

Step 8

Now stand your character up, and try pushing it over.

Step 9

You could make more wobblers and decorate them as aliens or circus performers—or use your own ideas!

How does it work?

The wobbler has a very low center of gravity, since its top half is light but the base is heavy. When another force acts on it (for instance, when you push it), gravity will pull it back to a point directly above the point where its mass is concentrated. This is called its state of equilibrium.

Parachute Jump

It's time to parachute some cork commandos behind enemy lines. Which parachute works best?

You will need

- **String**
- **Materials for making the parachutes, such as plastic shopping bags, paper, tinfoil, and tissue paper**
- **A pencil and ruler**
- **Scissors**
- **Tape**
- **A cork**
- **A small eye hook**
- **A kitchen scale**
- **A sturdy chair**
- **A stopwatch (on a cell phone or watch)**

Step 1

Using scissors, cut a 12 inch (30 cm) square from a plastic shopping bag.

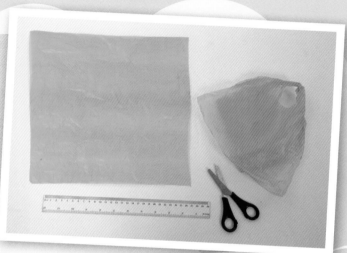

Step 2

Cut four pieces of string 30 cm (12 inches) long. Tie one end of each piece of string to a corner of the square of plastic.

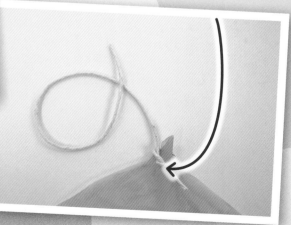

59

Step 3

Twist an eye hook into one end of a cork.

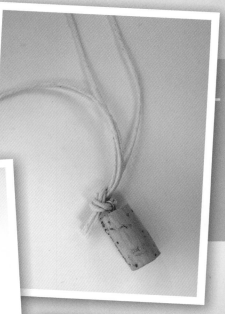

Step 4

Hold the strings from the parachute together, and tie them to the screw.

Step 5

Stand on a chair, reach as high as you can, and drop the parachute.

Step 6

Try making parachutes of different sizes and materials. You can also try using other objects as weights, such as plastic toys. Drop them from the same height.

Step 7

Make a chart to see which features make the best parachutes. Time your test drops. Measure the size and weight of the parachute.

Size	Weight	Material	Time

How does it work?

Parachutes work by creating air resistance. This is a kind of friction that works against the pull of gravity. The best way to increase air resistance is to make as large a surface area as possible. So the size of your parachute will probably make more of a difference than anything else.

Out in space

Astronauts wear spacesuits whenever they leave a spacecraft. In space, there is no air to breath, no air pressure, and it is very cold. Without protection, an astronaut would quickly die. When an astronaut gets out of a spacecraft while in space to do important tasks, it's called a spacewalk. A spacesuit keeps astronauts from getting too cold or hot, provides them with the water they need to drink, ... with oxygen to breathe

Down to Earth

All objects attract each other with gravity, and the larger the object, the larger the force. The Earth is huge so has a strong gravitational pull.

You will need

- A styrofoam cup
- Water
- A stepladder or something you can stand on safely
- An old ballpoint pen
- Small plastic bucket
- Somewhere outside to do the experiments

Experiment 1

Step 1

Make a small hole with the pen in the side of the cup near the base.

Step 2

Fill the cup with water. See how the water runs out.

WARNING!
Ask an adult to help you when you're using the stepladder.

Step 3

Cover the hole with your finger and fill the cup again. Stand on the stepladder, and drop the cup of water.

How does it work?

Gravity makes the cup and the water accelerate down at the same rate. They fall together, and the water stays in the cup until they hit the ground.

Experiment 2

Step 1

Half fill your bucket with water.

Step 2

Outside, swing the bucket forward and back. Increase the swing, and make sure you don't spill any water.

Step 3

When you get near the top of the swing, try going straight over the top in a complete circle!

How does it work?

When you swing the bucket, you apply a centrifugal force to the water in addition to gravity. The faster you swing, the greater the centrifugal force. When it's great enough, the water will stay in the bucket, regardless of gravity.

Jet Propulsion

Did you know that the first jet engine was invented in the first century AD? Find out how a jet engine works in this easy experiment.

Experiment 1

Step 1

Thread the fishing line or string through the straw.

Step 2

Find a big space, preferably outdoors. Fill the balloon with air, then put the bulldog clip on the neck to keep the air in.

Step 3

Fix the straw to the balloon with tape. Tie each end of the line to something fixed, at least 20 feet (6 m) apart.

Step 4

Release the clip!

How does it work?

The air inside the balloon is under pressure caused by the balloon trying to go back to its original shape. When the clip is released, air escapes through the neck, and the balloon is pushed in the opposite direction.

Experiment 2

Step 1

Open the top flaps of the fruit juice carton and make small holes in them. Attach a loop of string between the flaps and another to the exact middle of the first string.

Step 2

Make a hole in the front of the carton with the ballpoint pen, at the bottom on the left. Make a similar hole on the other side.

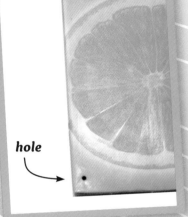

hole

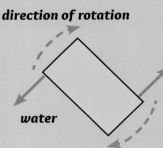

Step 3

From here, it's best to work outside! Cover the holes with your finger and thumb, and fill the carton with water. You might need an assistant for this.

Step 4

Hold the carton up by the string, then uncover the holes.

How does it work?

The force of the escaping water on opposite sides drives the carton around in a circle, with the string acting as a pivot. We're using gravity and water to make jet propulsion!

direction of rotation

water

Sink or Swim?

If we drop a piece of metal into water, it sinks. So how is it that a ship made of material that's heavier than water can float?

You will need

- Plasticine clay
- Paper clips
- Water
- An egg
- A pitcher
- Salt
- A tablespoon

Experiment 1

Step 1

Knead a piece of plasticine into the size and shape of a golf ball.

Step 2

Fill the pitcher with water, then drop the clay ball into it. It sinks!

Step 3

Take the ball out of the water. Dry it, then form it into a hollow shape. Carefully lower the plasticine shape into the water again.

Step 4

Your boat will even carry cargo!

How does it work?

A ball of plasticine clay is denser than water, so in Step 2, it sinks. By spreading the clay out over a larger area, you are changing its density, so the plasticine in Step 3 floats.

Experiment 2

Step 1

Half fill the pitcher with water and add about six tablespoons of salt. Stir it well to dissolve the salt.

Step 2

Top up with plain water. Pour the water over a spoon so as not to mix it with the salt water.

Step 3

Carefully lower the egg into the glass using the spoon. Try not to disturb the water!

Step 4

The egg floats halfway down the pitcher!

How does it work?

The egg is denser than plain water but less dense than salt water. The egg has buoyancy in the salt water but not in the plain water, so it floats where the two kinds of water meet.

Thread Reel Racer

We store energy, such as gas, so it is available when we need it. Our bodies also take in forms of stored energy when we eat. Here's how to make a toy that uses stored energy move.

You will need

- A long pencil
- A rubber band
- An empty thread reel
- A piece of candle
- A paper clip
- A craft knife

Step 1

Get an adult to cut a slice of candle. Make a hole in the middle.

WARNING!
Ask an adult to cut the candle—don't do this yourself.

Step 2

Push the rubber band through the thread reel, then attach the paper clip.

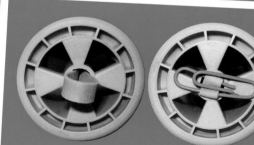

Step 3

Thread the rubber band through the candle.

70

Step 4

Put the pencil through the rubber band, and wind it up as tightly as you can without breaking the band.

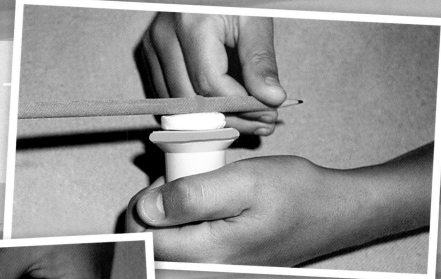

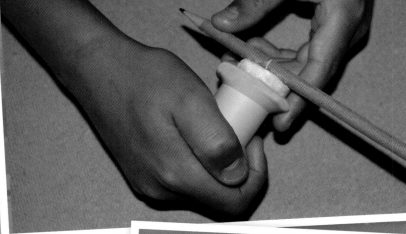

Step 5

When the rubber band feels tight, put the whole thing on a level surface and release.

Step 6

How far will it go?

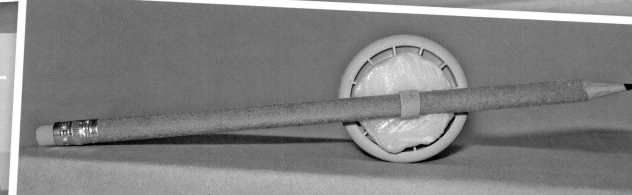

How does it work?

We call the energy used to twist the rubber band in Step 4 *potential energy*. When we release the racer, the rubber tries to return to its normal length, and as it straightens, some of its potential energy is converted to movement (*kinetic energy*).

Air Force

How do planes stay in the sky? What invisible forces are at work to help them fly?

You will need

- A styrofoam sheet such as a pizza tray
- Plasticine clay
- A black marker pen
- Scissors
- A glue stick
- Colored paper
- A pencil, paint, and brush
- Tracing paper
- An adult with a craft knife

Step 1

Copy these three shapes onto a sheet of styrofoam. Carefully cut around the shapes with scissors. Ask an adult to cut out the two slots with a craft knife.

WARNING!
Ask an adult to cut the slots in the plane with a craft knife.

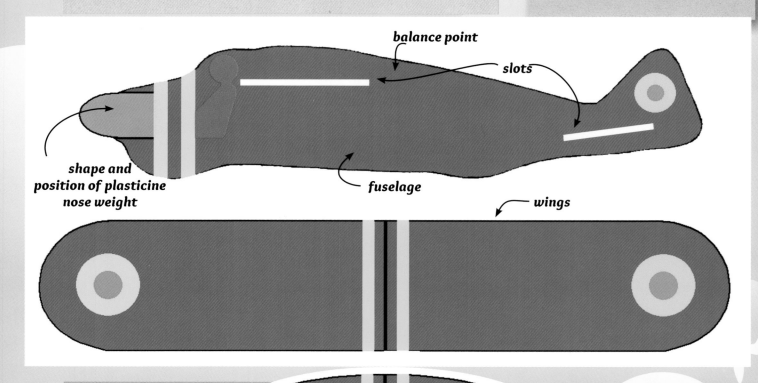

balance point

slots

shape and position of plasticine nose weight

fuselage

wings

horizontal stabilizer

Step 2

Paint the flat shapes first. Apply markings after paint is dry using colored paper shapes and a glue stick.

Step 3

Add details such as the body panels and cockpit with a black marker pen.

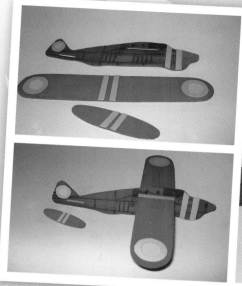

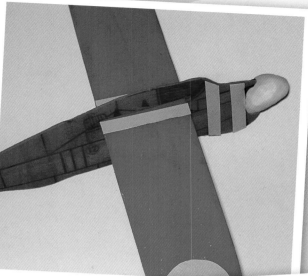

Step 4

Check that all paint and glue is dry. Push wings and tail into the slots. Use the clay to make a nose weight.

Step 5

Adjust the position of the nose weight until the plane is balanced on both sides. Launch the plane with the nose slightly down. Good flying!

How does it work?

The plane needs the forward motion of the launch to thrust it through the air. The wings passing through air convert this force to lift, opposing the force of gravity. The horizontal stabilizer and tail fin stabilize the plane, keeping it at the right angle to stay up. If the plane loses forward movement through the air, it loses lift and drops.

73

Balloon Fun

We've used balloons a lot in our experiments but there are still things they can show us. Here are two more forces at work.

You will need

- Balloons
- One very large balloon
- A permanent marker
- String
- An assistant
- A woolen sweater
- Kitchen scale

Experiment 1

Step 1

Here's a big, empty balloon. It weighs just 0.7 ounces (20 g).

Step 2

Blow it up and weigh it again. The balloon seems to weigh about the same.

If you can, use an electronic scale. They are better at weighing tiny amounts.

Step 3

Your assistant takes the balloon and—while you're not looking—whacks you on the back with it!

How does it work?

The balloon doesn't seem to weigh anymore after we've blown it up than it did before. But it feels heavier than the empty balloon would when it hits us, because it carries the mass of the air inside it as well as the rubber of the balloon, all propelled by your assistant.

74

Experiment 2

Step 1

Blow up two balloons and tie their necks. Attach strings.

Step 2

With the strings at the top, draw a face on each balloon. Use a permanent marker so it doesn't smudge.

Step 3

Find somewhere to hang them up—a doorway is ideal for this. Let them hang about 2 inches (5 cm) apart, and see where they settle.

Step 4

Rub the faces of the balloons with the woolen sweater.

Step 5

Let them hang free again, and see how they behave.

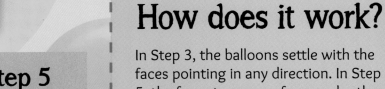

How does it work?

In Step 3, the balloons settle with the faces pointing in any direction. In Step 5, the faces turn away from each other. Rubbing a balloon with woolen fabric produces an electrostatic charge on it. A similar charge on both balloons means that they will repel each other. The force should be strongest where the rubbing occurred, and so the faces turn away from each other.

BRIGHT IDEAS

In this chapter, we will explore the science surrounding the fastest thing in the universe—light! It travels at 186,000 miles (300,000 km) per second, in case you were wondering …

This picture shows a "stellar nursery" far across our galaxy. This is where stars are born, and the light takes thousands of years to reach Earth. So when you are looking at the stars, you are actually looking at the past!

Kaleidoscope

Make thousands of crazy, colorful patterns with your own kaleidoscope!

Step 1

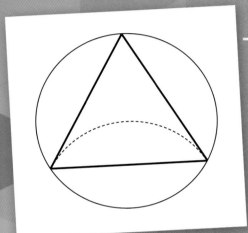

Draw around the bottom of a paper towel tube onto a piece of paper. Open your compass so the point is on the circle and the pencil is exactly in the middle. Draw the shape shown with dotted lines. Mark in the base of the triangle. Open your compass to this line, then mark the third point of your triangle. Draw the triangle.

Step 2

Using a ruler, draw a rectangle the same length as the cardboard tube on the back of the mirror cardstock. Mark off three parts with the same width as the sides of the triangle you drew.

Step 3

Fold the mirror cardstock along the lines to form a triangular shape. The mirrored side should be on the inside. Slide it into the paper towel tube.

78

Step 4

Draw around the end of the tube onto a piece of black cardstock. Cut out the circle, using scissors.

Step 5

Stick the circle on the end of the tube with tape. Make a hole in the center.

Step 6

Turn over the tube. Stretch plastic wrap over this end, and fix it in place with tape.

Step 7

Cut a 1 inch- (25 mm-) wide strip of thin cardstock, and tape it around the end of the tube. Make sure it stands out a little from the end of the tube.

Step 8

Place some small pieces of colored cellophane on top of the plastic wrap.

Step 9

Draw around the bottom of the tube onto tracing paper. Cut out the circle, leaving a gap of about half an inch (1 cm). Cut small flaps around the edge. Place this shape over the top of the tube, then stick down the flaps with tape.

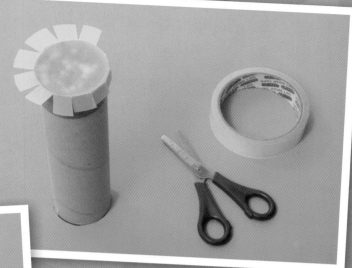

Step 10

Decorate the tube with wrapping paper.

Step 11

Hold your kaleidoscope up to the light. Look through the hole and turn the tube. What do you see?

How does it work?

Light normally travels in a straight line. When it hits a mirror, it bounces off it in a different direction—this is called reflection. In a kaleidoscope, the light bounces around back and forth off the walls, creating many, many reflections of the colorful objects inside.

Hall of Mirrors

Have you ever been to the fair and looked in the carnival mirrors? They can make you look tall, short, wide or just plain weird! Here's how to make your own.

You will need

- A big shiny spoon
- 2 shallow cardboard boxes (e.g., shoebox lids)
- Four sheets of thin mirror cardstock
- Tape
- Scissors
- A craft knife
- Adhesive putty
- Thin black cardstock

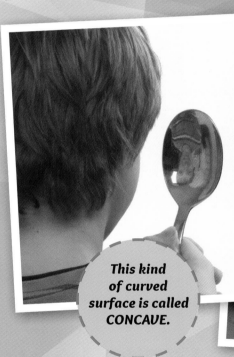

This kind of curved surface is called CONCAVE.

This kind of curved surface is called CONVEX.

Step 1

Look at your reflection in a shiny spoon. What differences can you see between the reflections on each side?

Step 2

Let's make some mirrors to see those effects more clearly! Line the sides of a shallow cardboard box with black cardstock. Strengthen the corners with tape.

81

Step 3

Measure the inside of your box. Then cut a piece of thin mirror cardstock or plastic to the same width as the box but about 2 inches (5 cm) longer.

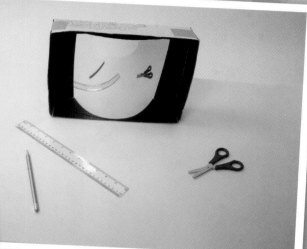

Step 4

Bend the mirror and place it in the box. The sides should hold it securely.

Step 5

Cut a hole in the bottom of another box with scissors, leaving half an inch (12 mm) around the edge.

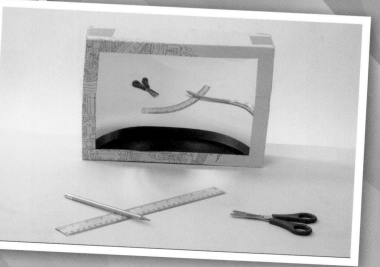

Step 6

Prepare the mirror cardstock as before, but this time turn it the other way up.

Step 7

Ask an adult to score some mirror cardstock in different ways, using a craft knife.

Step 8

Stick the pieces of mirror cardstock onto black or colored cardstock using adhesive putty. Decorate the frames with colored paper. Now you have four mirrors for your hall of mirrors!

How does it work?

When light hits the surface of a mirror, the direction of the reflected light depends on the shape of the mirror. If a mirror bulges outward, it is called convex. Convex mirrors make objects look stretched. If a mirror bends inward, it is called concave. Concave mirrors make objects look smaller—or even flip them upside down! It depends on how far away you stand.

A Box Full of Sky

Have you ever wondered why the sky is blue when it is lit by the sun, which looks orange? Here is a simple experiment that explains it all.

Step 1

Fill the container three-quarters full of water. Add a little milk to the water, and stir it with a spoon.

Step 2

Position the flashlight on some books, so that it shines through the middle part of the water.

Step 3

Shine the flashlight through the water, but stand to the side of the beam. Keep adding milk to the water and stirring. After a while, the light will turn blue.

Step 4

Now stand in front of the flashlight. The beam will look orange!

How does it work?

When the sun shines, light of different colors is bounced around by air particles. Blue-colored light gets bounced around more than light of any other color, so the sky looks blue. The same thing happens in our experiment when light is bounced around by the milk. But when you stand in front of the flashlight and look at the beam, it mimics sunrise and sunset and looks orange. This is because red and yellow light is bounced around much less than blue. Remember, don't look directly at the sun—it can damage your eyes.

Amazing Aurora

The spectacular light display shown here is called the aurora borealis (or Northern Lights). It's a display that can be seen at night in places near the North Pole (the aurora australis can be seen at the South Pole). Auroras happen because of charged particles that come from the sun. These particles sometimes hit the Earth, but we are protected by Earth's magnetic field. However, there are weak spots in the magnetic field near the poles. Here, the charged particles react with particles in the air and create the aurora borealis, an amazing light show!

3-D Glasses

View amazing 3-D pictures through your own handmade glasses!

You will need

- **Cardstock or cardboard**
- **Red and blue-green colored plastic (called Mylar) from a craft store**
- **Tape**
- **A glue stick**
- **Scissors**
- **The 3-D images on pages 90–91**

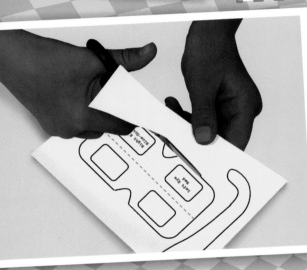

Step 1

Copy the template opposite, and cut out the three parts of the glasses. Score along the dotted lines.

Step 2

Cut out two rectangles of colored plastic—one should be blue-green and the other red. Tape them to the glasses.

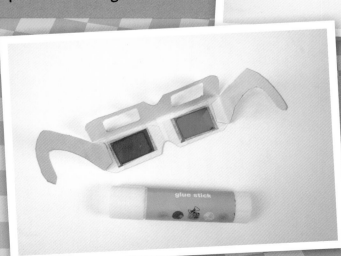

Step 3

Fold the earpiece flaps along the dotted lines and fix to the frame with a glue stick or tape.

Step 4

Fold the frame down to seal in the lenses and the earpiece flaps. Secure them with tape.

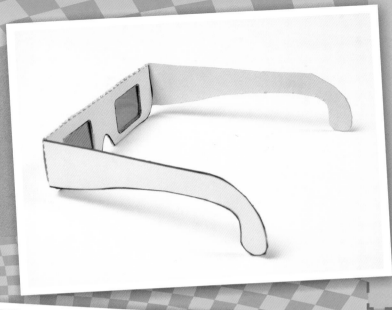

How does it work?

The blue-green lens makes it hard to see blue and green, but you can still see red. The red lens does the opposite. Your brain tries to make sense of the different images each eye is seeing by turning them into a 3-D picture!

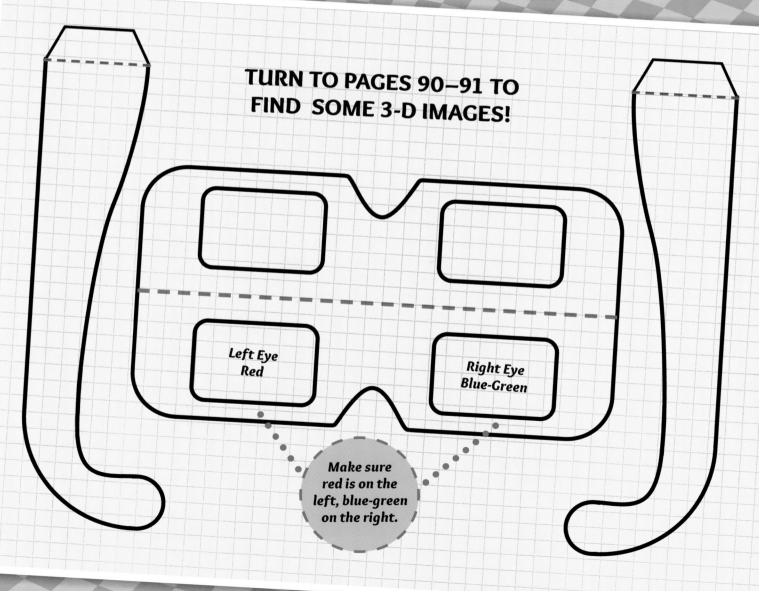

TURN TO PAGES 90–91 TO FIND SOME 3-D IMAGES!

Left Eye
Red

Right Eye
Blue-Green

Make sure red is on the left, blue-green on the right.

Trick Your Eyes!

Sometimes what you see is not all it seems. Play tricks on your brain and eyes with these fun optical illusions!

Step 1

Look at the rabbit in the middle of this picture. Does it look as if the spots are rippling and moving?

Step 2

Focus your eyes on the circle in the middle of this image. Can you see the other circle turning around it?

How does it work?

A phenomenon such as an optical illusion tricks us because the different cells and receptors in our eyes receive and process information at different rates. As a result, the brain can sometimes receive a false image based on the information arriving at varying speeds.

93

Light Top

Make a terrific top that changes color before your eyes as it spins around!

You will need

- **Old CDs or DVDs**
- **Marbles**
- **Tape and glue stick**
- **A hard surface**
- **A pencil**
- **Scissors**
- **Pens or paints**
- **Colored paper**

Step 1

Draw around a CD or DVD on colored paper. Cut out several circles. Also cut out the holes in the middle.

Step 2

Stick a paper disk to the CD or DVD with a glue stick.

Step 3

Fix a marble in the central hole of the disk with small strips of tape. Test spinning it on a hard surface, such as a kitchen countertop.

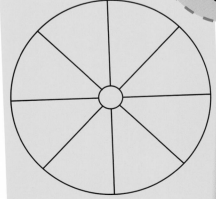

Step 4

Use more paper or colored pens or paints to make bold patterns on the disk.

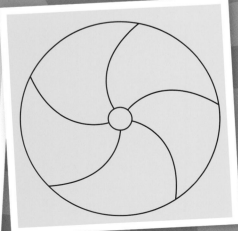

Step 5

Now try spinning your first disk.

Can you see new colors when the disk spins?

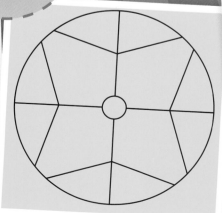

Here are some patterns to copy. Or you could make up some of your own!

Step 6

Here's a way to make neat segments. Fold a circle three times. Then cut along the last fold with the scissors.

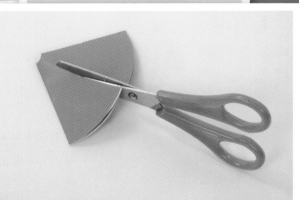

What happens if you make a spiral pattern?

How does it work?

When the top whirls around really fast, you can see all the colors, but your brain can't separate them. So what you see is a blend of all the colors mixed together.

Make Your Own Zoetrope

Have you ever dreamed of being an animator? You can make a start here by creating your first-ever moving picture!

You will need

- A circular box (such as a cheese box) with a lid
- Modeling clay
- A map tack
- A small button
- A piece of cork
- Tape
- A ruler
- Scissors
- A pencil and pen
- Black paper and white paper
- Colored paper

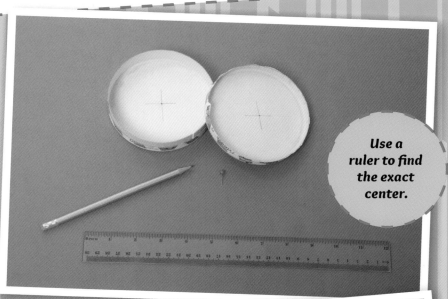

Use a ruler to find the exact center.

Step 1

Poke a hole in the center of a circular box and its lid with a map tack.

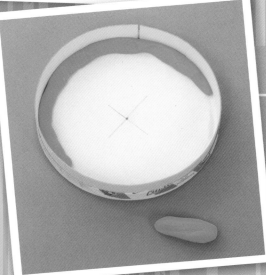

Step 2

Put some modeling clay around the edge of the inside of the box, to add weight.

Step 3

Push the map tack through the lid, through the hole in a button, through the bottom of the base, and into a cork beneath. The box should now spin freely on the lid.

Step 4

Cut a piece of black paper about 2.5 inches (6.5 cm) high that will fit around the inside edge of the lid.

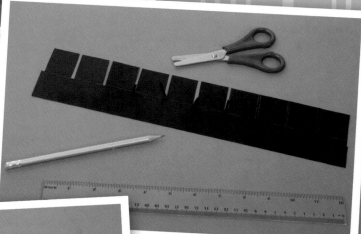

Step 5

Draw lines along the black paper about 1 inch (3 cm) apart. Following those guidelines, cut slots about 1.5 inches (4 cm) deep.

Step 6

Stick the black paper in place with tape. Then cut a piece of white paper, 1¼ inches (3 cm) wide to fit inside it. Don't stick it down yet!

A repeated action that joins up at the beginning and end will work well.

Step 7

Draw guidelines along the white paper 1¼ inches (3 cm) apart. Draw a series of pictures in the "frames" that you have marked out. Put the paper inside the box.

You could decorate the outside of the box with colored paper.

Step 8

Spin the zoetrope and watch your animation through the slits.

How does it work?

When you spin the zoetrope, you can see each of the pictures one at a time in very quick succession. Your brain tries to make sense of what your eyes take in. It interprets these rapidly changing pictures as movement, so you see a continuous moving picture.

Rainbow Maker

You don't need to wait for rain to see a rainbow anymore. Here is how to make a nice, dry one indoors. You may not find a pot of gold at the end, though!

You will need

- Some old CDs
- A sunny day, or if this is not possible, a flashlight
- A window with curtains or blinds
- White paper

Step 1

Find a sunny window. Close the blind or curtain, but leave a little gap to let the direct sunlight in.

Step 2

Hold a CD, shiny side up, in the beam of sunlight.

Step 3

Reflect the light onto a piece of white paper.

Step 4

Change the angle of the CD. You will see a variety of different rainbow patterns.

Step 5

You can use a flashlight if it's not a sunny day, but the rainbows might not be as bright.

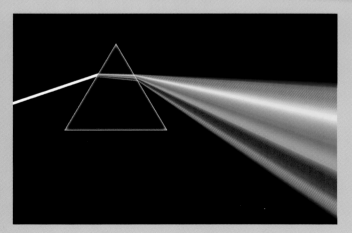

How does it work?

When white light passes through a triangular prism, it splits into all the different colors of the rainbow. The surface of a CD is made of plastic with lots of tiny ridges above a mirrored surface. These act like lots of tiny prisms arranged in a circle, so when light hits the surface of the CD, it makes a rainbow.

Night Lights

Before the invention of the electric light, the Earth would have looked very different at night from how it looks now. This image is a satellite picture of Earth from space taken at night. It shows a clear outline of the United States.

The brightest lights show us where the major cities and towns are. Cities tend to grow up along coastlines and transportation networks, such as rivers, roads, and railroads.

Pepper's Ghost

This experiment is part science and part magic trick, and all about not necessarily believing what we see. The effect is named after John Pepper, the nineteenth-century scientist who perfected it. We are going to reveal the secret of Pepper's ghost ...

You will need

- A cardboard box—about 12 x 9 x 15 inches (30 x 22 x 40 cm)
- Tape
- Sheets of strong black paper
- Clear plastic—the same size as one face of box
- A tea light with holder
- Matches
- Cardboard tube—about 3 in (8 cm) diameter, 6 in (15 cm) tall
- A sheet of cardstock
- A glass of water
- Glue stick
- Paints and brushes

Step 1

Measure 1 inch (3 cm) in from the edges of one side of the box, then cut a window.

Step 2

Using the glue and tape, line the inside of the box with black paper, except for the window. Fix the plastic over the window with tape.

Step 3

Ask an adult to help you cut a piece out of the cardboard tube, about a quarter of its *circumference*, from top to base. Line the inside of the rest of the tube with black paper.

Step 4

Light the tea light and place it in front of the box. Fill the glass with water. Find the position of the virtual image of the tea light, and put the glass inside the box.

Step 5

Position the tube so that the candle is totally screened from the front.

Step 6

Now view the effect from the front. The candle should seem to be still burning underwater!

How does it work?

Normally, we can see straight through clear plastic, and in daylight, it appears as if all the light goes through. In fact, a small amount is reflected, but in daylight, it's too faint to see.

In this experiment, we've positioned the glass so that the candle's reflection in the plastic is in the exact same place. This optical illusion tricks your brain into thinking that the candle is burning underwater.

Light Trap

This experiment shows you how fiber optics works. Light can only travel in straight lines, but it's possible to bounce it inside of a material like water. You can use this technique to make it travel along a stream of water!

You will need

- A glass or glass container
- Water
- A little milk
- A plastic bottle
- Tin foil
- A kitchen sink
- Flashlight
- Tape
- A small screwdriver
- A friend to help you
- A kitchen you can make dark

Experiment 1

Step 1

Fill a glass container with water. Add a few drops of milk.

Step 2

Put some tin foil around the end of your flashlight, then make a slit in it.

Step 3

Darken the room. With the slit horizontal, shine the flashlight up through the side of the glass, adjusting the angle until light reflects down from the surface of the water.

Experiment 2

Step 1

Cover the bottle with foil, using tape to hold it in place. Leave the base of the bottle uncovered.

Step 2

Make a hole in the side of the bottle near the top.

Step 3

Cover the hole with your thumb and fill the bottle with water.

Step 4

Replace the screw top. Keep your thumb over the hole. Turn the bottle upside down. Hold the lit flashlight against the base.

Step 5

Get your friend to turn off the lights. Remove your thumb from the hole. The water escaping will pick up light from the flashlight.

How does it work?

In Experiment 1, if the angle between the water and the light is great enough, light is reflected back. In Experiment 2, because of the large angle at which the light hits the boundary between water and air, it is reflected back into the water. When it hits the other side of the stream, the same thing happens. This is called total internal reflection. The light only escapes when the water stream hits the sink and scatters.

Color Mix-Up

We know that when we combine two different colors of paint, we get a third one—but what about mixing colored light?

You will need

- **White cardstock**
- **Flashlight**
- **Paints and brushes**
- **Clear plastic sheet in different colors—buy from a craft store or try candy wrappers**
- **A notebook and pencil**
- **A darkened room**

Experiment 1

Step 1

Paint three patches of thick color—blue, red, and green.

Step 2

While the paint is wet, use a clean, dry brush to blend the edges of the patches together. First blend blue into red.

Step 3

Then clean your brush and blend red into green.

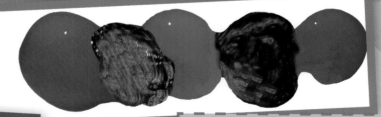

Step 4

Finally blend all three colors together.

How does it work?

The blends between the three colors are muddy and less bright than the colors that make them. Paint is made to absorb all the other colors of light and only reflects its own.

Experiment 2

Step 1

This time we're going to use colored plastic to filter the light from a flashlight.

Step 2

Work in a darkened room. Shine your flashlight onto white cardstock. Try the colored filters one at a time, then try combining them. Write down the results.

Step 3

Try red and blue. You should see magenta (pink or purple red).

Step 4

Blue and green makes cyan (turquoise).

Step 5

Green and red make yellow.

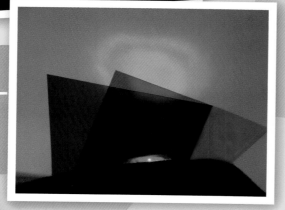

How does it work?

The results are quite different from those produced by using paint. Mixing our red and blue paint produced a dull brownish purple. When we add red and blue light, we get a bright magenta.

Seeing Around Corners

The periscope is a device that uses mirrors to let us see around things. It's a good way to see over the heads of crowds! We're going to make a simple periscope.

Step 1

Remove any plastic spout, and seal the box with tape. Measure the depth of the box (D), and mark the same distance up the side.

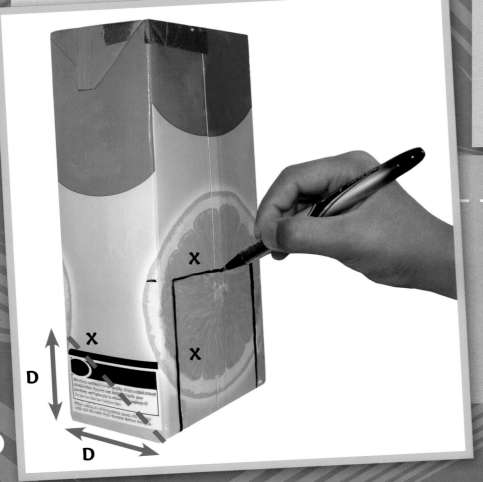

Step 2

Measure the diagonal (X). Using the ruler, draw the outline of a square flap on the bottom of the front of the box (black line). Be careful to use the same measurement (X) for the height and width of the flap.

Step 3

Carefully cut three sides of the flap and fold inward. Use tape to fix the flap at a 45° slant.

Step 4

Cut a flap at the top of the box on the other side, the same size (X by X) as before. Fix this flap, again at a 45° slant, with tape.

Step 5

Stick one mirror to each flap with some glue.

Step 6

Now test your periscope!

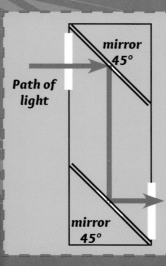

How does it work?

mirror 45°

Path of light

mirror 45°

Light travels in straight lines. The first mirror changes the direction of the light by reflecting it. Then, the second mirror changes it back, parallel to its original path. Submarines use periscopes so that the crew can see above the waves while the submarine remains safely under the water.

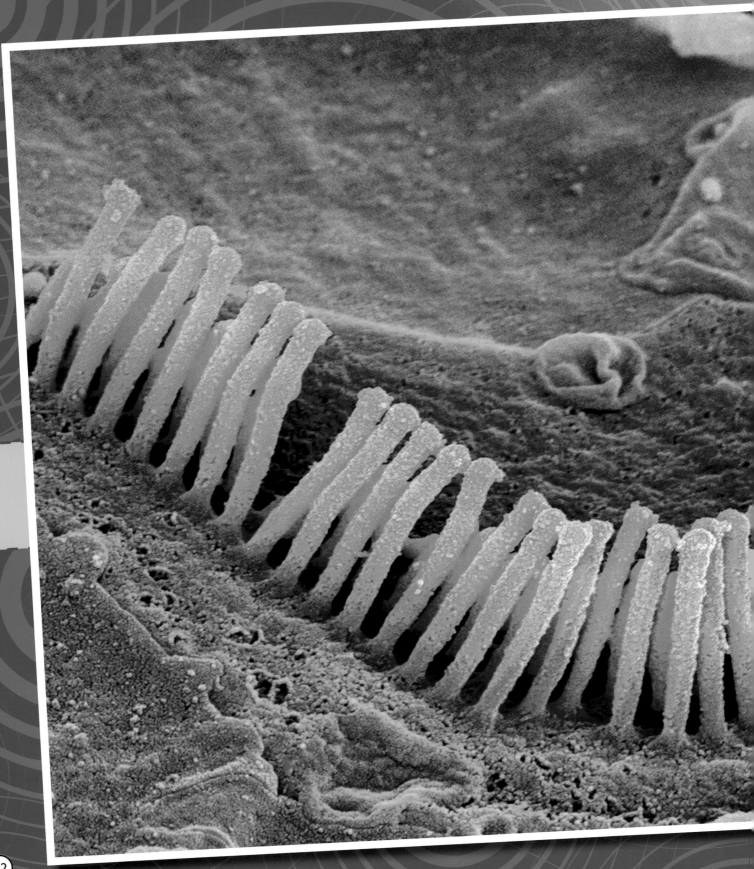

SUPER SONIC

Did you know that everything you hear is a vibration? Get ready to learn about the science of sound!

This photo shows the inside of an ear that has been magnified 21,000 times! Sound vibration makes the liquid in the inner ear move in waves, which makes the hairs sway. Then they turn that movement into an electrical signal, which is sent to your brain!

Make Your Own Drum Set

March to the beat of your own drum with this noisy experiment. Using household objects, you can create a drum set that works just like the real thing!

You will need

- Containers such as small glass jars, cans, and plastic buckets
- Materials to make the drum skins, such as plastic shopping bags, paper, cloth, tin foil, and balloons
- Materials to make drumsticks, such as chopsticks, skewers, and wooden spoons
- A metal saucepan lid
- Some string
- Rubber bands
- Marker pens
- Scissors
- Tape
- A glue stick
- Colorful paper

Which containers and drum skins work the best?

Step 1

Draw around a can onto a plastic shopping bag. Then cut out the circle with scissors, adding a half-inch (10 mm) margin around the edge.

Step 2

Stick the sheet in place with pieces of tape, pulling the skin tight as you go. Then decorate the can by gluing on colored paper.

Adding tape to the sticks will make a softer sound.

Step 3

Test your first drum with two drumsticks!

Step 4

Cut down one side of a balloon with a pair of scissors, to make a stretchy skin. Pull it over the top of a small container. Hold it in place with a rubber band.

The rubber band should be tight.

Step 5

Make some more drums from other materials. Each should sound slightly different. Finally, make a cymbal by tying a string around the knob on a saucepan lid. Hang it above the rest of your drum set.

How does it work?

When you hit a drum, it creates a vibration, which is what we hear as a noise. Lots of different things can change the pattern of the vibrations, which changes the noise that you hear: the materials you use, the size of the drum, how tight the skin is stretched, and even where you hit it.

Paper Popper

You will need

- A sheet of paper measuring 16 x 12 inches (40 x 30 cm)

Step 1

Fold the paper in half along the long side, then open it out again.

Step 2

Fold the corners into the crease line in the middle, like this.

Step 3

Fold it again along the original central crease.

117

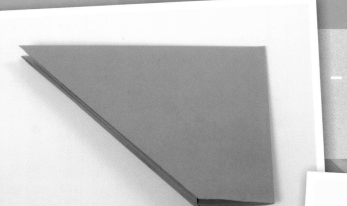

Step 4

Fold the pointed ends together.

Step 5

Fold the top left corner down like this.

Step 6

Turn it over, and fold the flap down in the same way on the other side.

Step 7

The paper should look like this.

Hold this end!

118

Step 8

Hold the noisemaker like this.

Step 9

Swing the noisemaker down like this. It should make a sound like cracking a whip!

How does it work?

Swinging the noisemaker downward compresses (squashes) the air inside it. The air is suddenly freed when the inner fold opens out. That causes a rapid decompression: a small explosion of air!

Dancing Flame

We all know you can make a flame flutter by blowing on it, but did you know that you can make a flame dance with the power of sound?

Step 1

Using scissors, cut the bottom off a plastic bottle.

WARNING!
Ask an adult to help you cut the bottom off the plastic bottle.

Step 2

Cut a square of plastic from a plastic bag that is at least half an inch (1 cm) bigger than the base of the bottle. Fix it to the base with a rubber band.

Step 3

Light the candle. Position the bottle so that the neck points toward the flame.

Step 4

Tap the plastic sheet without moving the bottle. The candle flame will flicker with the sound!

How does it work?

All sounds are vibrations in the air. We don't normally see what is happening when the air vibrates—we just hear it as the vibrations reach our ears. However, the small flame in our experiment is so sensitive to air movement, that we can clearly see it move in response to vibrations traveling through the air.

What a Noise!

When an object vibrates, it causes movement in the air particles called sound waves. These particles bump into the particles close to them, which makes them vibrate, too, causing them to bump into more air particles. This movement keeps going until they run out of energy. If your ear is in range of the vibrations, you hear the sound. The howler monkey shown here on the right is known for its extremely loud howls, which can travel 3 miles (5 km) through dense rain forest.

Funky Bone Vibrations

We already know that vibrations can travel through air. They can also travel through other materials, such as ... your head!

Step 1

Bang the fork on a table so that it makes a ringing noise.

Don't risk damaging an expensive table—any hard surface will do.

Step 2

Note how loud the noise is.

Make sure you hold the pointy end away from you!

Step 3

Now bang the fork again. This time, hold it behind your ear, pressing it against the bone. Is it louder or quieter?

Step 4

Now bang the fork and grip the handle in your teeth. This time it should be really loud!

How does it work?

This experiment shows you that sound travels better through bone than air. This is important because you have tiny little bones in your ear that vibrate, stimulating nerve signals to the brain to tell you that you are hearing something. If bone didn't conduct sound so well, you wouldn't be able to hear as well as you do.

Where's That Sound?

Why do we need two ears and not just one? This fun experiment shows you why, by confusing your sense of hearing!

You will need

- Two pieces of plastic tubing 20 inches (50 cm) long, from a hardware store
- Two funnels
- Masking tape
- Scissors
- A headband
- An assistant

Step 1

Attach two funnels to pieces of plastic tubing. You might need to hold them in place with tape.

Step 2

Tape the two pieces of tubing together.

Step 3

Tape the tubes onto a headband.

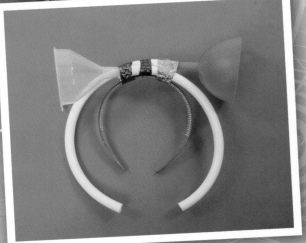

Step 4

Put the headset on your head, and hold the ends of the tubes, one in each ear.

Step 5

Close your eyes. Ask your assistant to make a variety of noises in different places.

Step 6

Can you tell where each noise was coming from?

How does it work?

We can usually tell whether a sound is to our left or right based on how loudly we hear it in each ear. The tubes take sounds to the wrong ears!

127

Paper Kazoo

Here is how you can make the easiest, silliest instrument in the world. All you need is a simple piece of paper!

You will need

- Paper
- Scissors
- A ruler
- A pencil

Step 1

Rule a line on a piece of paper about 1 inch (2.5 cm) wide and 4 inches (10 cm) long. Then cut the shape out with scissors.

Step 2

Fold the paper in half lengthwise, then fold the ends back.

Step 3

Using scissors, cut a small, V-shaped notch into the middle of the central fold.

Step 4

Hold it to your mouth like this, and squeeze air between your lips.

Step 5

Try making longer and shorter kazoos! Does the sound change?

Step 6

Can you play a tune with your kazoos? Get your friends to join in!

How does it work?

Blowing between the two sheets of paper makes them vibrate and creates the buzzing sound that you can hear. Reed instruments such as saxophones and clarinets work in exactly the same way.

Cup Screech

This experiment might make your friends hold their ears! It makes a very loud noise—a noise that drives some people up the wall.

You will need

- A piece of string about 15 inches (40 cm) long
- A plastic cup
- An old ballpoint pen
- An eraser
- Some water

Place the eraser under the cup to support it as you make the hole.

Step 1

Make a hole in the bottom of a plastic cup using an old ballpoint pen.

Step 2

Thread the string through the hole, and tie a knot in the end to keep it from coming out.

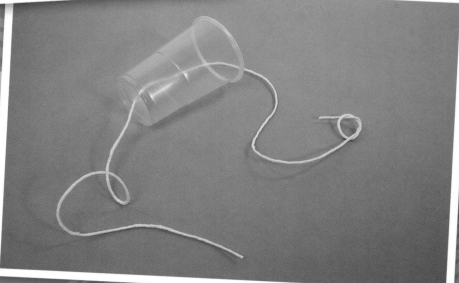

130

Step 3

Wet the string with water.

Step 4

Hold the cup in one hand like this.

Step 5

With your other hand, slide the wet string between your thumb and forefinger. With a little practice, you should be able to make a horrible screeching sound!

How does it work?

Your fingers sliding across the wet string make it vibrate, and the cup amplifies this, creating a screeching noise. Why do we find this screeching unpleasant? Some scientists think that it is because it is similar to the sound of a scream.

Whale Song

Did you know that sound travels at different speeds, depending on the temperature of the air and what material it is traveling through? For example, in water, sound travels much farther than it does through the air. In fact, up to four times faster! Whales can communicate with each other across long distances by making low-pitched noises. They can be heard "singing" by other whales hundreds of miles away.

Secret Sounds

Sound travels to our ears through the air by making the molecules in the air vibrate, but it can also pass through solid materials in the same way. We are going to show that sound can pass through solid materials.

You will need

- A friend to help you
- String
- Metal objects such as silverware or a coat hanger
- 2 clean yogurt cups
- Hammer
- Nail

Experiment 1

Step 1

Tie the ends of two pieces of string to metal objects.

Step 2

Hold the end of the string and gently put your finger in your ear. Swing the object so that it bangs against a wall. Now try using both objects.

How does it work?

When the object is hit, it vibrates, making a sound that we can hear normally. As we are suspending the objects on taut string, the vibration will travel up the string, making it vibrate. Because we have our fingers pressed into our ears, we can't hear normally through the air, but we can hear the transmitted vibration coming up the string.

Step 1

Get your string and two clean yogurt cups ready to make a great telephone.

Knot the string inside each cup. Pull the string tight between the cups.

Step 2

Ask an adult to make a hole in the base of each cup with a hammer and nail, then fix a long piece of string between the cups.

Step 3

Give the other cup to a friend. Stand some distance apart, keep the string tight, and listen or speak!

Step 4

How long can you make the string and still hear the person at the other end?

135

Seeing Sound

We can't actually see sound, but we can see its effect! In this experiment, we are going to show that sound travels in waves.

You will need

- Large bowl
- Plastic wrap
- Rice
- 2 clean plastic bottles
- Plastic sheet, cut from a shopping bag
- Tape
- Feathers, tissue paper
- Container used for potato chips
- Hammer and nail
- Scissors

Experiment 1

Step 1

Stretch some plastic wrap over the top of the bowl. Sprinkle some dry rice over the surface of the plastic wrap.

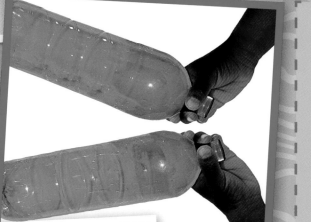

Step 2

Bang two plastic bottles together near the bowl.

How does it work?

The sound of the plastic bottles banging together transmits through the air in waves and causes the plastic wrap to vibrate, bouncing the rice up and down.

Step 3

What happens to the rice? What happens when you bang the bottles farther away?

136

Experiment 2

Step 1

Ask an adult to make a hole in the closed end of the container. We used a nail and hammer.

Step 2

Take the piece of shopping bag plastic, and stretch it over the open end of the tube. Hold the piece of plastic firmly in place with some tape.

Step 3

Point the end with the hole toward the feathers or little pieces of tissue paper. Tap the plastic at the other end sharply.

How does it work?

When you hit the plastic, the sound waves pass down the tube and out through the hole, moving the feathers. This is the shock wave that causes damage in an explosion.

In Tune?

You will need

- **Several similar glass bottles**
- **Water, food coloring (optional)**
- **Paper and pencil**
- **Stick or ruler**

Sound is produced in lots of ways. Here's a method of producing different sounds using the same equipment. We are going to see how you can make different types of sound.

Step 1

Fill the bottles with water to different levels. Put the bottles in a line and in order—most water to least water. We've colored ours, but it's not necessary for the experiment.

Step 2

Test them for pitch by striking each bottle (gently) with a stick. Strike each bottle in the same place.

Step 3

Use the same set of bottles. Now blow across the top of each bottle one by one. Try and get a clear note.

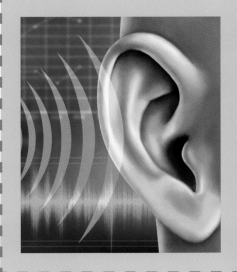

How does it work?

Sound is made by creating vibrations in a material. These vibrations are carried through the air to our ears as waves.

In Step 2, the sound is made by a sharp blow of the stick, making the combination of water and glass vibrate. The more water there is in the bottle, the lower the pitch, and the less water, the higher the pitch.

In Step 3, the sound is made by vibrating a volume of air. The greater the volume of air, the lower the pitch, and the smaller the volume of air, the higher—exactly the opposite result to Step 2.

139

Bouncing Sound

Sound can be reflected in much the same way as light. It's what happens when you hear an echo. We are going to find out whether sound follows the same rules as light when it is reflected.

You will need

- A friend to help you
- 2 cardboard tubes (from tin foil or similar)
- Ticking alarm clock
- Notebook
- Pencil
- Stiff cardstock
- Shoe box
- Scissors
- Tape

Step 1

Cut a round hole in the side of the box, then fit a tube to it.

Step 2

Put the box and tube on a table. Place the sound source (the clock) inside the box.

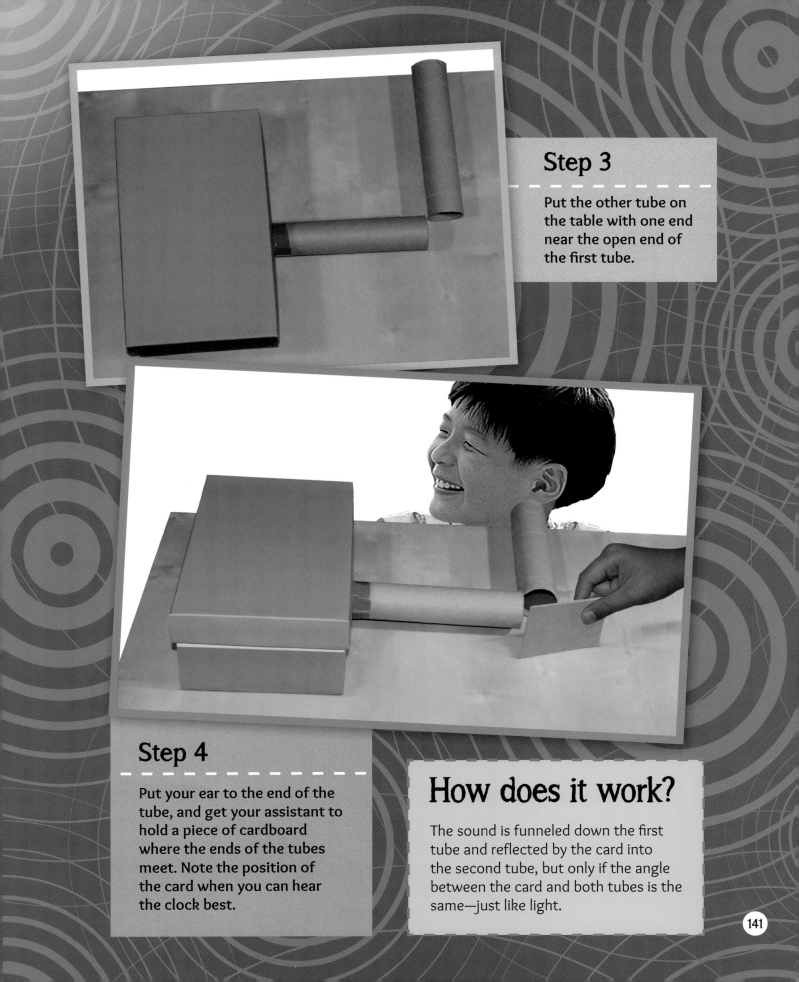

Step 3

Put the other tube on the table with one end near the open end of the first tube.

Step 4

Put your ear to the end of the tube, and get your assistant to hold a piece of cardboard where the ends of the tubes meet. Note the position of the card when you can hear the clock best.

How does it work?

The sound is funneled down the first tube and reflected by the card into the second tube, but only if the angle between the card and both tubes is the same—just like light.

IT'S ALIVE

The world is full of fascinating and amazing living things. The area of science that looks at living things is called biology.

Honeybees are fascinating creatures. They use an expressive "waggle dance" to tell other bees the direction and distance of good sources of food.

Growing Seeds

You will need

- Paper towel
- Thick cardboard
- 4 clean, shallow food trays
- Quick-germinating seeds, such as alfalfa
- Water
- A refrigerator

Many plants spread themselves by scattering seeds. A seed contains a new plant and enough food for it to start growing. We are going to find out what else a seed needs to germinate—water, light, warmth? You'll need to collect some food trays for this project.

Step 1

Put three or four thicknesses of paper towel in the bottom of each tray. Scatter the same number of seeds in each tray. Label them A, B, C, D. Wet the paper towels in trays A, B, and C.

A
has water, light, and warmth

B
has no warmth and no light

C
has no light

D
has no water

144

Step 2

Put trays A and D near a window in a warm room.

Step 3

Cover tray C with thick cardboard to keep the light out, and put it with A and D.

Step 4

Put tray B in the refrigerator to give no warmth.

Step 5

Check the trays daily. After five days, the seeds should look very different.

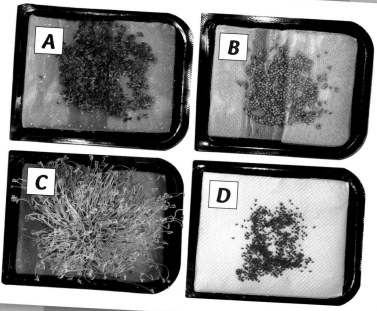

How does it work?

Seeds won't germinate without water, but they don't need light. Without warmth, they grow more slowly or don't germinate at all.

145

Which Way Is Up?

Have you ever wondered why a plant's roots always grow down and its leaves grow up? We are going to germinate some seeds in different positions to see which way the roots grow.

Step 1

Cut a piece of paper towel to fit around the sides of the jar, so that it fits snugly against the sides.

Start with four bean seeds from the package.

Step 2

Find the black scar on each seed. Put one seed in each jar, between the glass and the paper towel. Make each bean lie in a different direction. The first with the scar up; the second with it down; the third with it to the left; the fourth to the right.

The black scar is where the bean was attached to its pod.

Step 3

Put about 1 inch (25 mm) of water in each jar. It should soak into the paper to reach the seeds. Keep the water at this level.

Step 4

After they have germinated, you could turn the seeds so that the roots are pointing upward, and see what happens!

How does it work?

The roots and the shoots always grow from the same point on the seed, but they react to gravity. Roots grow with gravity; shoots grow against gravity.

Silly Celery

Have you ever seen a plant with blue leaves? Here's how you can dye plants different colors.

You will need

- Sticks of celery with leaves still on
- 2 glasses
- Blue and red food coloring
- Water
- A countertop
- Kitchen scissors

Step 1

Pour water into a glass so it is a third full. Add a small amount of food coloring.

Step 2

Trim the bottom of a stick of celery so that it is about 6 inches (15 cm) long. Leave the leaves on.

Step 3

Put the end of the celery into the liquid in the glass. Leave the glass in a safe place, where it won't be moved.

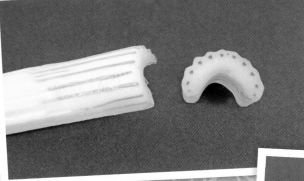

Step 4

After one day, cut across the base of the celery with scissors. You will see lines of color rising up the stalk.

Step 5

Split another stick of celery. Put colored water in two glasses. Allow each part of the split stalk to stand in a glass.

How does it work?

Plants take up water from the soil through their roots. The water travels all the way up the stems to the leaves, through tubes called the xylem. If you put dye in the water, then that will be taken up, too. Try the experiment with a white flower to see the petals change their color!

Step 6

The following day you will have multicolored celery! Cut back the stalks to check.

149

The Perfect Place for Plants

You will need

- **4 same-size seedlings**
- **4 similar containers**
- **Compost, sand, gravel, soil**
- **Water**
- **Labels**
- **Notebook and pen**

Have you ever wondered if plants like some kinds of soil more than others? By testing with seedlings, we try to find out where they grow best. We are going to see how seedlings develop when planted in different types of growing material.

You will need

- **4 same-size seedlings**
- **4 similar containers**
- **Compost, sand, gravel, soil**
- **Water**
- **Labels**
- **Notebook and pen**

Step 1

Put compost, sand, gravel, and garden soil into similar sized containers. We have used clean glass jars.

Step 2

Transplant four seedlings from their pots to the containers. Keep in identical conditions with light and warmth. Give each plant half a cup of water. Label each jar.

compost

sand

gravel

soil

compost   sand   gravel   soil

Step 3

After a week, you should be able to see clearly which plants are thriving or failing. Do you know why?

compost

Step 4

Remove the BEST plant from the jar to check the root structure. Notice that both the leaves and the roots are developing well. This plant likes the conditions you have provided.

How does it work?

Results should prove that plants prefer a mixed material to grow in, such as garden soil or compost. They will not grow as well in sand or gravel, which provides no nutrients.

Step 5

Remove the WORST plant from the jar to check the root structure. The plant is weak. Notice that both the leaves and the roots are not developing well. This plant does not like the conditions you have provided.

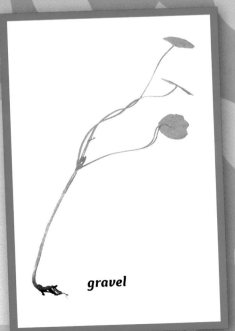

gravel

151

Stone Flowers

These unusual plants are known as living stones, stone flowers, or pebble plants. They are one of the world's most fascinating plants! They look so much like the pebbles and stones among which they grow in Africa, that they were only discovered by scientists in 1811.

House for a Louse

You probably have a house that's dry, warm, and light—but would that suit other animals? We are going to find out what kind of conditions wood lice like to live in!

You will need

- 5 similar-sized cardboard boxes
- 4 cardboard tubes
- 2 plastic bags
- 2 pieces of cardboard
- Plastic wrap
- Paper towels
- Tape
- Marker pen
- 15 live wood lice (look under stones)
- Scissors
- Water
- Notebook
- Thumbtack

Step 1

Place a cardboard tube on the long side of a tissue box. Draw around the tube with a marker pen.

Step 2

Cut out the circle with scissors. Repeat the process on three more boxes. On the last box, you will need to mark and cut out a hole in each side.

Step 3

Cut out the top of all five boxes, leaving a ½ inch (12 mm) border around the edge. Mark the boxes A, B, C, D, and E.

WARNING!
Ask an adult to help you cut the boxes.

Step 4

Line the bases of all the boxes inside with plastic sheet cut from a bag, then put in two layers of paper towel. Dampen the paper in boxes A and B. Stretch plastic wrap over two of the boxes, A and C. Use cardboard, cut to the right size, to cover two more boxes, B and D. Use tape to fix the covers.

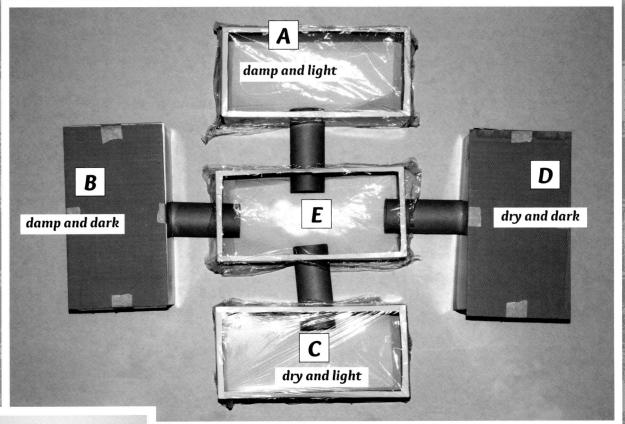

A damp and light

B damp and dark

D dry and dark

E

C dry and light

Step 5

Push the tubes into each box, and connect them as shown in the photograph above. Fix the tubes with tape. Make pin holes in the sides of all boxes for air (see inset picture).

Step 6

Place the wood lice in box E, then cover box with plastic wrap. Over a period of four days, carefully check the numbers of wood lice in each outer box to see which one they prefer! Make notes of results.

IMPORTANT!
Put the wood lice back where you found them once you have finished observing them!

How does it work?

Like plants, animals are adapted to different living conditions—what suits one could kill another.

A Wormery

We know that worms live under the ground. What do they do there? And why are they popular with gardeners? We are going to make a wormery.

You will need

- 2 sheets of clear plastic, 12 inches (300 mm) square
- 3 pieces of wood 1 x 2 inches (25 x 50 mm) cut into: 1 piece 12 inches (300 mm) and 2 pieces 11 inches (275 mm) long
- Strong waterproof tape
- All-purpose glue
- Scissors
- Sand and soil
- Leaves and grass
- Earthworms

Step 1

Assemble the pieces of the wormery as shown here.

Step 2

Lay one sheet of plastic on a table; put the longest piece of wood at the base. Fix with glue. Add the two sides.

short pieces at the sides

long piece of wood at the base

Step 3

Allow the glue to dry completely. Spread more glue on the surface of the wooden frame to fix the second piece of plastic. This completes the box. But you could tape all around the frame for extra strength.

Step 4

Add soil and sand in 1 inch (25 mm) layers. Dampen the sand with water. Put the worms on the top layer with some leaves and tufts of grass for food. Keep the soil damp, but do not overwater.

Step 5

Observe the wormery over several days and weeks. Make notes about the results.

soil
sand
soil
sand
soil
sand
soil
sand

worms move the layers around   *worms drag the leaves underground*

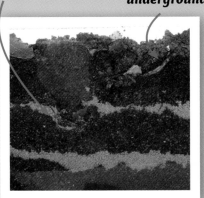

How does it work?

The worms mix up the soil as they move around and feed. They also break up lumps of soil and dry leaves, which become food for plants. Their burrows allow air into the soil, which also helps break down plant material. All these activities improve the soil, so most gardeners like worms in their garden.

IMPORTANT!
When your experiment is finished, return your worms to the place you found them.

Bug Hunters

Time to get up close to some creepy-crawlies! They might be tiny, but these fascinating little creatures are a very important part of nature.

You will need

- A small patch of ground you can dig up
- Trowels
- A clean glass jar
- Grass or leaves
- A large glass or plastic lid

Step 1

Find a flat area of ground where you have permission to dig. Make a hole with a trowel, deep enough to hold your glass jar upright.

Step 2

Put some grass and leaves in the hole.

Step 3

Place the jar in the hole without a lid, standing it upright to make a trap.

Step 4

Cover the trap with grass and leaves.

Step 5

Protect the trap from the rain by covering the hole with a glass or plastic lid.

Step 6

Check your trap the following day to see what's in it! Can you identify the bugs and creepy-crawlies? Check on the Web or in your library to find the names and habits of these creatures.

How does it work?

When bugs fall into your trap, they find it hard to climb back out again because the glass sides are so smooth. See if you can identify the bugs that you have caught. Look at them through a magnifying glass to see them in greater detail. Make sure you return them to the outdoors when you have had a good look. Leaving bugs in the trap for a long time is cruel and could kill them.

Spotted!

Animals will go to great lengths to survive. One way in which they do this is called camouflage. Camouflage is a way that animals have of resembling the habitat in which they live. The pygmy seahorse would probably get first prize for best camouflage. Can you see it hidden here among the coral? It is so effective at hiding that scientists did not discover it until the piece of coral where it lived was being examined in a laboratory.

Yeast Balloon

Yeast is a tiny microorganism that has a massive impact on your life. See the amazing power of yeast by using it to blow up a balloon.

Step 1

Pour 10 fluid ounces (300 ml) of water into a bowl. Add a package of dry yeast and 2 tablespoons of sugar. Stir the mixture until the yeast and sugar have dissolved.

Step 2

Pour the mixture into the bottle.

Step 3

Warm up the balloon in your hands. To soften the rubber more, grip the ends of the balloon and stretch it.

Step 4

Stretch the open end of the balloon over the neck of the bottle. Make sure it is pulled down over the screw threads on the top of the bottle to prevent air from leaking.

Step 5

Leave the bottle upright with the balloon fitted for one hour, then check the result!

Step 6

Leave the bottle undisturbed overnight. In the morning, the balloon will be even bigger!

How does it work?

The yeast needs sugar and water to activate it, and then it begins to respire (breathe). As it does this, it creates the gas carbon dioxide, which is what blows up the balloon. Yeast is what we use to make bread rise, so it is a very important little creature!

163

Bottle Bird Feeder

Attention all animal lovers! These ingenious feeders will attract birds and squirrels to your yard. Then you can observe them and learn all about them!

WARNING!
Ask an adult to help you cut the bottle.

Step 1

Ask an adult to help you cut a circular hole about 2 inches (5 cm) across in the side of a half-gallon (2-liter) bottle, using scissors.

Step 2

Tie some string around the top of the bottle.

Step 3

Pour some birdseed into your bottle. The seed should almost reach the hole when the bottle stands upright.

Step 4

Hang up your bird feeder bottle outside where the birds can feed safely. It needs to be high, so they won't feel threatened by cats and other predators.

Peanut Cones

You will need

- **A pine cone**
- **String**
- **Peanut butter**
- **A spoon**
- **Birdseed**
- **Popcorn**
- **Needle and thread**

Step 1

Tie a piece of string to the top of a pine cone.

Step 2

Smother the pine cone with peanut butter, using a spoon. Then roll it in birdseed and hang it up in the yard.

WARNING!
Ask an adult to help you make the popcorn and use a needle and thread.

Step 3

Get an adult to help you make some plain popcorn, then use a needle and thread to connect about 50 pieces of popcorn together. Hang it up outside. The birds will love it!

If your bird feeder starts to look old or get moldy, recycle it and make a nice new one!

How does it work?

If you hang your feeders within view of your window, you can observe the birds from indoors so that they aren't disturbed. A lot of people put feeders out to help the birds make it through the cold winter, when it can be hard for birds to find food. Watch carefully and see if you can identify different species. See how they interact with each other. Is there a pecking order?

DNA from Strawberries

DNA is the thing that makes you YOU. It is found in every one of your cells and contains the instructions that your body has followed to make you the way you are. Every living creature has different DNA. Now you can see the DNA of strawberries in your very own kitchen!

You will need

- A freezer
- 3 strawberries
- Salt
- A measuring cup
- Scissors
- Paper towel
- A plastic bag
- 2 plastic cups
- Laundry detergent (liquid or powdered)
- A glass
- Ice cubes
- 2 big bowls
- A fork
- A teaspoon
- A toothpick
- Ice-cold rubbing alcohol (ask an adult for help)

Step 1

Put the rubbing alcohol in the freezer at least an hour before you do this experiment.

Step 2

Remove the stems from the strawberries, then break them up using a fork.

Step 3

Put the pieces into a measuring cup. Add one teaspoon of detergent to half a cup of warm water, and pour the mixture over the fruit.

Step 4

Stand the cup in a bowl of warm water. The detergent and warm water will start breaking up the strawberry cells. Wait 12 minutes, stirring often.

Step 5

Next, stand the cup in a bowl of ice cubes for 5 minutes.

Step 6

Cut the corner off the plastic bag and line it with the paper towel. Then pour the strawberry mush through, so that the liquid with the DNA collects in a cup.

Step 7

Add a quarter teaspoon of salt to the collected liquid. Mix it well.

Step 8

Now pour some of the mixture into a clear glass, so it is about a third full. Ask an adult to pour in an equal amount of ice-cold rubbing alcohol, and then rock the glass gently.

Step 9

Let the glass stand for a few minutes. A cloudy patch should form at the top of the mixture. It may look bubbly or whitish. This is strawberry DNA! You can remove it with a toothpick. It will look like clear slime! Isn't it incredible to think that the slime contains all the information for making a strawberry plant?

How does it work?

To get to a strawberry's DNA, first we mash the fruit to break open its cells. Then we separate the cells into their parts, using the enzymes in laundry detergent. The ice stops the detergent from breaking apart the DNA itself. Then we filter the mixture, and the liquid we are left with is called the "supernatent," which contains the DNA. Finally, adding salt and rubbing alcohol makes the DNA break apart from the rest of the solution and rise to the top.

Ready for My Close-Up

Scientists use a special piece of equipment called a microscope to look at things very closely. Like a magnifying glass, it makes small objects appear much larger. This photo shows a close-up of the scales on a blue morpho butterfly. Its wings are covered in bright blue-and-green shimmery scales. These scales reflect light differently depending on its direction.

Bending a Chicken Bone

Everybody knows that bones are hard. Or are they? Freak out your family and friends by turning a chicken bone soft and rubbery.

You will need

- A large clean jar with a lid
- A chicken bone; a "drumstick" works best
- Vinegar

Step 1

Save the bone from a drumstick after a chicken meal.

Step 2

Remove any meat from the bone, and rinse it under running water.

172

Step 3

Notice how hard and stiff the bone is. Bones contain a mineral called calcium to make them hard.

Now you have to wait for the "magic" to happen ...

Step 4

Put the bone in the jar, then pour vinegar in so it covers the bone completely.

Step 5

After four days, open the jar and take out the bone. Rinse it with water, and see how bendable it is! Pour the vinegar down the sink.

How does it work?

The vinegar dissolves the calcium in the bone. The calcium is what made the bone strong and hard, and without it, the bone becomes soft and bendable. This is why it's important for you to get enough calcium in your diet—trying to walk around with bendy bones wouldn't be much fun!

How Big Are Your Lungs?

I'll huff, and I'll puff, and I'll ... test my lung capacity! Try this simple experiment to see exactly how much air your lungs can hold.

You will need

- An empty half-gallon (2-liter) plastic bottle
- A medium-size bowl
- A big bowl
- A flexible straw
- Water
- Lots of breath!

Step 1

Fill a bottle with water all the way to the top.

Step 2

Screw the cap on.

Step 3

Put the smaller bowl in the bigger bowl. Add water to the smaller bowl until it is ¾ full.

Step 4

Hold the bottle in the bowl with the neck in the water, then take off the cap.

Keep the neck of the bottle under the water!

Step 5

Put the end of the straw in the bottle. Blow out one big breath!

Step 6

You will be able to see how much air you can store in your lungs! Ask a friend or family member to try the experiment. Who has the biggest lung capacity?

How does it work?

When you blow down, the air you breath out forces out the water that was in the bottle. The empty space is exactly equal to how much air your lungs can hold.

Seeing Things

So far, we have experimented with some of the living things in the world around us. But we are alive, too, and we can also experiment on ourselves! We are going to learn a little about how our eyes work and how using two eyes is often better than one!

You will need

- Small table
- Large sheet of paper
- 3 different-colored markers
- A jar lid
- Scissors
- Thin cardstock
- A pencil
- Glue stick
- String

Experiment 1

Step 1

Draw a target on paper, and put it flat on a table.

Step 2

COVER ONE EYE. To test your aim, hold a marker with the top removed, at arm's length. Try to drop it on the center of the target.

COVER THE OTHER EYE. Repeat the test, and try to hit the target with the next marker.

USE BOTH EYES. Repeat test with last marker.

Experiment 2

Step 1

Draw around a jar lid with a marker. Cut out two disks from cardstock to make a spinner.

WARNING!
Ask an adult to help you cut out the disks.

Step 2

Draw a simple birdcage on one disk and a blackbird on the other one. Stick the disks together, back to back, with one drawing upside down.

Step 3

Make a hole on each side of the card, and tie a string to each hole. Holding the strings, flip the card circle so that the strings twist over and over.

Step 4

Pull the strings tight, so that the disk spins back and forth quickly. As you watch, you will see the two drawings combine—now the bird is in the cage!

How does it work?

In Experiment 1, are some marks off target? Each eye sees things from a slightly different angle. The brain compares the two images and figures out how far away objects are. It cannot do this with one eye only.

In Experiment 2, an image of what we see remains in the eye for a fraction of a second after the object disappears. Because the movement of the card is so rapid, the image is still there when it has spun around, so we see both sides of the disk at once.

Mystery Box

Touch is another important sense we rely on to keep us safe. It lets us experience sensations like hot and cold, rough and smooth, wet and dry, soft and hard. See if your friends can identify hidden objects by touch alone.

You will need

- Cardboard box
- Scissors
- 2 old black socks
- Duct tape
- Box decoration—color markers
- Objects to put in the box
- Dishwashing gloves

Use the tape inside the box to fix sock "sleeve."

Step 1

Cut two holes in the sides of the cardboard box, big enough to get your fist through. Decorate the box with colored paper or marker pens.

Step 2

Cut the straight parts off of two old black socks (ask before you ruin Dad's best footwear!). Use strong tape to fix them on the inside of the box, so they make "sleeves" coming out of the box. Put your hands through the socks to feel the objects in the box without seeing them.

Step 3

Collect some objects, such as a spoon, a tennis ball, toys, fruit, a pencil, a thread reel, a pine cone, sunglasses, a slipper, a brush, tin foil, keys, an oven glove, and an empty matchbox.

Step 4

Put several things in the box at the same time, without anyone else seeing. You can either have two people playing using one hand each or one person using both hands.

Step 5

Ask how many items are in the box. To help them guess an object, ask questions: "Is it heavy?" "Is it light?" Discuss the texture of objects: smooth, rough, bumpy, soft, hard, and so on. Record results to see who gets the most right.

Wearing a pair of dishwashing gloves, each person takes another turn using different objects. Again, everyone tries to guess what is in the box this time. Is it harder with gloves on?

How does it work?

You can now judge what happens when you rely on your sense of touch alone. It's harder to recognize objects when you cannot see them.

HOT STUFF

Temperature can completely change the behavior of the materials around us, or in some cases, it can transform them completely. It's time to learn about the science of hot and cold!

Did you know that hot air is lighter than cold air? That is how a hot-air balloon flies!

Hot Topic: Conduction

Conduction is the way heat is carried through solid materials, for example, from a stove burner through the saucepan to the food. We are going to find out which materials are best at conducting heat.

Step 1

Ask an adult to help you heat some water.

WARNING!
Ask an adult to help you with boiling water.

Step 2

Put some hot water in the mug. Be careful!

182

Step 3

Stand the first object in the water. Hold the other end. See how long it takes to become warm.

Step 4

Fill the mug with hot water again, and try other things. This time we're testing a metal coat hanger.

Step 5

Now it's a plastic drinking straw.

Step 6

This is a wooden spoon.

How does it work?

Energy in the form of heat passes from one molecule to the next along the object. Metals conduct heat well and so are called good conductors. Nonmetals, like plastics and wood, are not good conductors and are called insulators.

Moving Story: Convection

The way that heat is carried through liquids and gases is called convection. An example of this is a radiator heating up a whole room. We are going to show a convection current in air by using smoke.

You will need

- Shoebox with a lid
- 2 paper towel tubes
- Tealight candle in a holder
- An ice pop stick
- Tape
- Scissors
- Thin cardstock
- Matches
- Thread

Step 1

Draw two circles on the lid of the shoebox, one toward each end. Draw around the end of the paper towel tube.

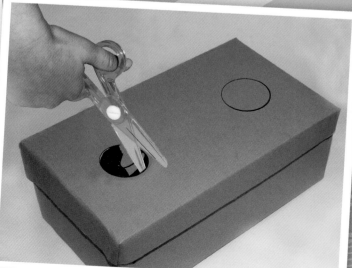

Step 2

Cut the holes out, and stick the tubes in place with tape.

Step 3

Light the tealight candle. Put it in the shoebox, so that it is under one of the tubes when the lid goes on.

Step 4

Light the end of the ice pop stick with a match. (Ask an adult to help.) Then blow the flame out.

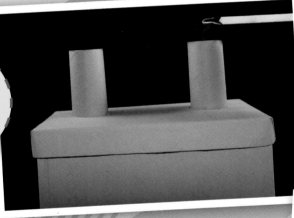

Step 5

Hold the glowing stick over the tube that doesn't have the tealight under it.

Step 6

Smoke goes down the tube and eventually comes out of the other. Make sure you blow out the candle once the experiment is over!

How does it work?

The candle flame heats the air, which rises up through the tube. Cooler air is heavier and is drawn down the other tube. Air travels through the box, drawing the smoke with it.

Warming Glow: Radiation

You will need

- **Thermometer**
- **Desk lamp**
- **Different materials cut into pieces of a similar size and shape: for instance, tin foil, white paper, bubble wrap, thin black cardstock**
- **Tape**

Radiation is the only form of heat that can travel through a vacuum. An example is the way heat gets to us from the sun, through space. The heat we feel from a desk lamp is also radiation. We are going to show how different substances absorb heat radiation.

Experiment 1

Step 1

Find a place to work where the temperature is fairly even. Keep away from direct sunlight and room heaters. Note the room temperature.

Step 2

We are using a desk lamp as a source of radiant heat. Put your thermometer under the lamp. Note the temperature rise after ten minutes.

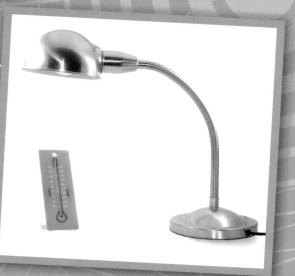

How does it work?

Heat is getting to the thermometer by radiation. It is a way in which heat travels as waves of energy.

Experiment 2

Step 1

Start with the thermometer at room temperature again. Wrap it in a fold of test material. This is tin foil, which is very thin aluminum sheet. Hold it in place with tape.

Step 2

Put the wrapped thermometer under the lamp. Note the temperature after 10 minutes, then at 10-minute intervals.

Keep the lamp at the same distance from the thermometer.

Step 3

Let the thermometer cool back to room temperature, then repeat with other materials. You can try combinations, too!

Step 4

Make a graph to show your results. It should show that shiny material insulates against radiant heat better than matt ones. Lighter material insulates better than darker material.

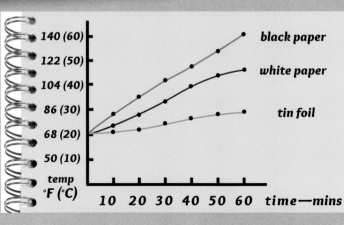

How does it work?

Dark, matt surfaces absorb these waves and soak up the heat. Light, shiny surfaces reflect the waves and stay cooler.

Blubber Glove

How does a walrus keep from freezing? Why are walruses covered in wobbling blubber? Let's make a blubber mitten and find out! You're going to find out for yourself how well fat works as an insulator.

You will need

- 4 sandwich bags
- Soft margarine at room temperature
- Dishwashing pan
- Ice cubes, spoons
- Hair elastics or string to put around your wrists
- Watch or clock that shows seconds
- A helper

Step 1

Scoop margarine into a plastic bag.

Step 2

Put one hand into another plastic bag. Use your left hand if you're right-handed, or your right hand if you're left-handed.

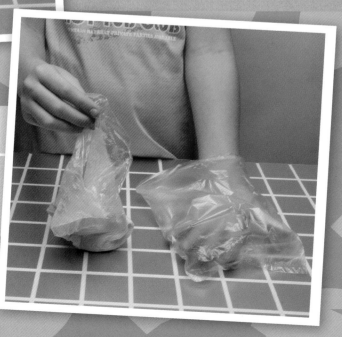

Step 3

Spread a thick layer of margarine over the outside of the bag. Now slide your hand inside its bag into the bag that already has margarine in. This is your "blubber mitten."

Step 4

Ask your friend to fasten the mitten with big hair elastics so that they don't slip off—but not too tight. Put two empty plastic bags on the other hand, then fasten these, too.

Step 5

Fill the bowl with cold water and ice cubes.

Step 6

Put both hands into the ice water. Don't let water into the bags. Use the watch to time how long you can keep each hand in the water before it gets uncomfortable.

How does it work?

The margarine insulates, keeping the warmth of your hand in rather than letting it pass to the water. Animals that live in very cold areas have thick layers of fat called blubber under their skin to keep their bodies warm.

Fire Show

Light travels roughly a million times quicker than sound. For that reason, you often see lightning before you hear thunder. Fireworks also appear in the sky before you hear their explosions. Fireworks have been around for centuries. In fact, the ancient Chinese used fireworks both as entertainment and to frighten their enemies in battle.

The Water Cycle

Nature has its own water recycling system we call the water cycle. We are going to see how water evaporates and condenses. Then we're going to make our own clouds!

You will need

- **Teakettle**
- **Hand mirror**
- **Oven gloves**
- **Clear, one-quart plastic bottle**
- **Matches (long ones are best)**

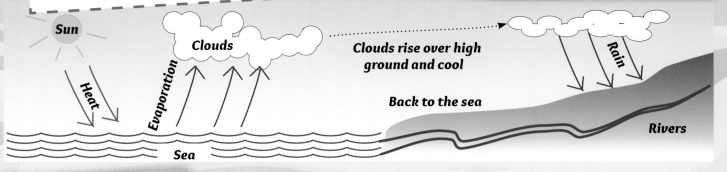

Sun

Clouds

Clouds rise over high ground and cool

Heat

Evaporation

Rain

Back to the sea

Rivers

Sea

Experiment 1

Step 1

Fill a teakettle half full of water and start heating.

Step 2

When it begins to boil, turn it off or take off the stove. Use oven gloves to hold the mirror in the steam.

Step 3

You should soon see water droplets form on the surface of the mirror.

How does it work?

A teakettle heats water until it starts to change from a liquid (water) to a vapor (steam). The steam is less dense than water and takes up more space, so it pushes its way out of the teakettle. Steam touching the surface of the mirror is quickly cooled and changes back to water.

Experiment 2

Step 1

Put enough warm water in a bottle to cover the bottom. Light a match and let it burn for a few seconds before blowing it out.

water level

WARNING!
Ask an adult to help you light the match.

Step 2

Immediately, hold the match in the neck of the bottle to catch as much smoke as you can.

Step 3

Quickly put the cap on the bottle so as not to lose any smoke.

Step 4

Squeeze the bottle eight or nine times (more may be necessary).

Step 5

When you release the bottle, you should see little clouds forming inside.

How does it work?

Some of the warm water evaporates inside the bottle. Releasing the pressure in the bottle slightly cools the air inside, so some of the water vapor changes back to liquid droplets. The smoke particles help them to form. Clouds are just collections of water droplets.

Bigger and Hotter: Expansion

When things get bigger, they are said to expand. Most liquids expand when they are heated, so we are going to use water to make our own thermometer.

You will need

- A plastic bottle
- A plastic drinking straw
- Plasticine clay
- Thermometer
- Warm water
- Food coloring
- Saucepan
- Stove

clay seal

Step 1

Fill the bottle to the brim with cool water mixed with a few drops of food coloring.

Step 2

Place the straw in the bottle, but leave most of the straw outside the bottle. Seal with plasticine clay.

Step 3

Put the bottle in a saucepan of warm water. Heat moves from the water in the pan to the water in the bottle. Water rises up the straw a little.

The water has risen from here

to here!

WARNING!
Ask an adult to help you. Do not let the water get too hot.

Step 4

Gently heat the pan. Get an adult to help you with this. As the water in the pan gets hotter, the water rises higher in the straw.

Step 5

Compare your thermometer with a commercial one. Make sure it's the kind that can go into very hot water. Use the readings from the commercial thermometer to label your new thermometer.

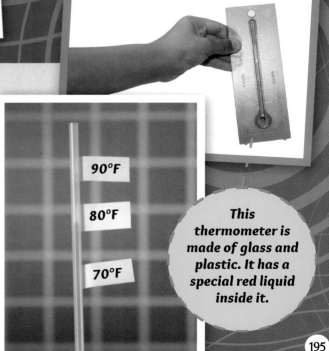

90°F

80°F

70°F

This thermometer is made of glass and plastic. It has a special red liquid inside it.

How does it work?

When the water is heated, it expands. The only way it can go is up the straw. The hotter it becomes, the more it expands, so the farther up the straw it goes.

195

Mighty Ice

In the last section, we said that most things contract when they cool. However, when water freezes, it expands! We are going to see why it is important not to let your water pipes freeze in the winter.

You will need

- 2 large plastic bottles
- 1 small plastic bottle
- Water
- Freezer

Experiment 1

Step 1

Fill the bottle to the top with cold water and put on the cap.

Step 2

Place it in the freezer. Leave it there overnight.

Step 3

By the next morning, the bottle will be swollen. It may even have split open!

bulge in bottle

196

How does it work?

When water freezes, it forms ice crystals, which occupy more space than water molecules. For the same volume, ice is less dense than water. Water is very unusual in this. Most liquids become more dense as they cool. Water is at its most dense at 39°F (4°C). An iceberg is lighter than the water it floats in, so that one-tenth of it is above the water.

Experiment 2

How can we check that one-tenth of floating ice is above the water? Iceberg shapes are very hard to measure!

Step 1

Use two plastic bottles, one a little smaller than the other. They need to be fairly straight-sided. Cut the top off the larger one. The smaller one should just fit inside it.

WARNING!
Cutting plastic is tricky! Ask an adult to help.

base of ice block

Step 2

Fill the smaller one with water but only as far as where it starts to narrow. Place it in the freezer overnight, standing upright.

4-6   8-12

Step 3

In the morning, get an adult to help you cut the bottle off the ice with scissors. Put some water in the larger bottle and float the ice block in it. You can now measure how much is standing out of the water.

Antifreeze

Have you ever wondered why we put salt on the roads when it's icy or snowing? We are going to see what effect adding salt to water has on the way it freezes.

You will need

- Two similar plastic bottles with screw tops
- Measuring cup and spoon
- Water
- Salt
- Freezer

Step 1

Make some salt solution. Add salt to water until no more will dissolve.

Step 2

Fill a bottle to the top with salt water and another with the same amount of plain cold water. Put them both in the freezer overnight.

plain water   salt solution

Step 3

In the morning, only the plain water has frozen.

plain water   salt solution

How does it work?

Impurities in water, in this case salt, lower the freezing point so the water remains liquid.

Ice Cube Trick

Here's a little trick you can try using ice.

Step 1

Put a cube of ice in a glass of plain water.

You will need

- A glass
- Ice cubes
- Water
- Salt
- Short piece of thread

Step 2

Pour a little salt onto the cube.

Step 3

Hang the end of a piece of thread so that it lies on the salty patch, and leave it for a few minutes.

Step 4

After a while, you'll be able to pick up the cube with the thread! Can you work out what's going on?

How does it work?

When the thread is placed on the ice cube, the salt melts the top of it. It eventually freezes around the string, causing it to stick.

Ice Castles

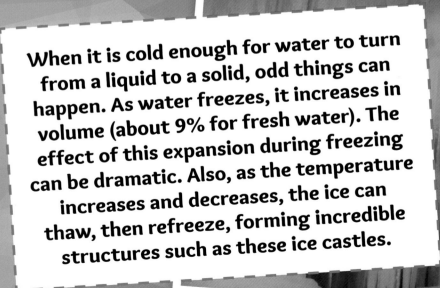

When it is cold enough for water to turn from a liquid to a solid, odd things can happen. As water freezes, it increases in volume (about 9% for fresh water). The effect of this expansion during freezing can be dramatic. Also, as the temperature increases and decreases, the ice can thaw, then refreeze, forming incredible structures such as these ice castles.

Disappearing Act

When we put certain things like salt or sugar into water, they seem to disappear. In fact, they are still there but have dissolved. We are going to see how temperature affects dissolving.

You will need

- Salt
- Small saucepan
- Two spoons
- Thermometer
- Water and stove
- Measuring cup

Step 1

Pour 16 fluid ounces (500 ml) of cold water into a measuring cup.

Step 2

Pour the water into a saucepan. Add salt, one spoonful at a time.

Step 3

Use another spoon to stir the water. Count how many spoonfuls can be added before no more will dissolve.

Step 4

Pour out the salty water. Now add a pint (500 ml) of warm water to the saucepan. Repeat with the water at different temperatures, using the same quantity of water and same size spoon each time.

See if the same thing happens with other solids. You could try different kinds of sugar, sand, or even chalk dust!

How does it work?

The hotter the water, the more salt it can hold in solution. When you let the water cool, the salt cannot stay in solution, and it falls out as salt crystals on the bottom of the pan.

sand

white sugar

crushed chalk

brown sugar

Mini Melt

In this chilly experiment, you can create a miniature iceberg to see how the density of water changes with temperature.

You will need

- Water
- A measuring cup
- A glass
- Food coloring
- 1/3 cup of vegetable oil
- An ice cube tray
- A freezer

Step 1

Prepare some special ice cubes by adding a few drops of food coloring to some water in a measuring cup.

Step 2

Fill an ice cube tray with the colored water. Put it in the freezer. It should be frozen in 2 to 3 hours.

Step 3

Fill a glass $1/3$ full with water.

Step 4

Pour in some vegetable oil until the glass is $2/3$ full.

Step 5

Take an ice cube out of the tray, then put it in the glass.

The water and oil form separate layers.

Step 6

Watch as the ice cube melts. What is happening?

Step 7

After about 30 minutes, the ice cube melts completely, the colored cold water stays at the bottom of the glass, and the oil is clear.

How does it work?

When water is in its liquid form, it is denser than oil, so the oil floats on top of it. However, when the water is frozen and becomes ice, it is less dense than the oil, so the ice floats on top of the oil.

Homemade Shrink Ray

Put your mad scientist hat on as you use the power of science to shrink everyday objects!

You will need

- An oven
- An oven glove
- A timer
- Snack bags (such as potato chip bags) made of plastic only
- Dishwashing liquid
- A paper towel
- Aluminum foil
- Brooch pins
- Superglue

Step 1

We are going to turn a full-size snack bag into a miniature one! Rinse out a bag with water and dishwashing liquid. Then ask an adult to preheat the oven to 475°F (245°C).

Step 2

Dry the bag with a paper towel.

Step 3

Wrap the bag in aluminum foil.

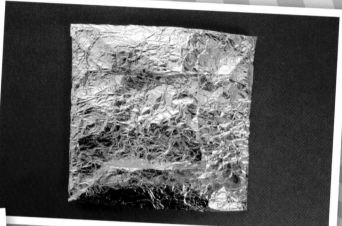

Step 4

Fold over the ends to make an envelope.

WARNING!
Ask an adult to help you use the hot oven.

Step 5

Ask an adult to help you place the aluminum foil envelope on the top shelf of the oven. Then close the oven door and check the temperature. Set the timer for two minutes. You need to stick to this time exactly.

Step 6

After two minutes, ask an adult to help you remove the envelope from the oven using an oven glove. Place the envelope on a heatproof surface.

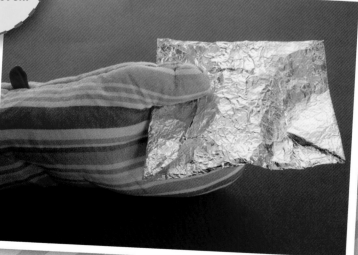

Step 7

Pat down the foil envelope with the oven glove, then let it cool.

Step 8

When it is cool, remove the shrunken bag from inside.

Step 9

Make gifts for your friends! Attach a brooch pin to the back of the miniature bags to make buttons.

How does it work?

The molecules making up the bag are in long chains called polymers, which are knotted tightly together. When the bag was made, it was heated and the polymers were stretched out flat. Heating up the empty bag releases the polymers, so they can scrunch up again.

Sun Burst

The sun is almost 93 million miles (145 million km) from the Earth. Without the sun, there would be no life on Earth. But get too close to this gigantic ball of fire, and you'll burn up! The sun often releases large amounts of gas into its atmosphere. These are known as solar flares. Some solar flares can be truly massive and contain impressive power. Sometimes, these powerful flares can even damage satellites orbiting the earth.

Solar Still

If you were ever stranded in the wilderness, this cool experiment could save your life by creating drinkable water from salt water!

You will need

- A sunny day!
- A large bowl
- A small jar or glass
- Plastic wrap
- A pitcher of water
- Salt
- A tablespoon
- Small, clean stones or marbles

Step 1

Put salt in a pitcher of water. Add about 4 tablespoons of salt to 1 quart (1 liter) of water. Stir thoroughly.

Step 2

Pour enough salty water into a large bowl so that it is about 2 inches (5 cm) deep.

Step 3

Place the small jar or glass in the center of the bowl of water. Make sure the top of the jar is above the salt water but well below the top of the large bowl. You'll probably need to put some small, clean stones or marbles in the glass to weigh it down and stop it from floating in the water.

212

Step 4

Stretch some plastic wrap over the top of the large bowl and make an airtight seal.

Step 5

Place a marble in the center of the plastic wrap, directly over the jar, to make it slope down into the middle.

Step 6

Put your solar still outside in the sun. Leave it for at least 4 hours. The longer you leave it out, the more water you'll collect.

Step 7

When you are ready to check your solar still, take off the plastic wrap and look at the water that's collected in the jar. Do you think it's salty or fresh? Taste it and see!

How does it work?

The heat from the sun causes water to evaporate from the bowl, leaving the salt behind. As this happens, the water vapor hits the plastic wrap and condenses back into liquid water again. The marble weighing the plastic down makes the water run down into the jar, thereby allowing you to collect fresh water!

Feeling Hot and Cold

Why is it that people feel temperature differently? When some people are snuggled up in coats, other people are walking around in T-shirts. This experiment tests how this is possible.

You will need

- 2 small containers, e.g., plastic pails
- A large bowl
- Hot water
- Cold water
- Ice cubes
- Room temperature water
- A towel

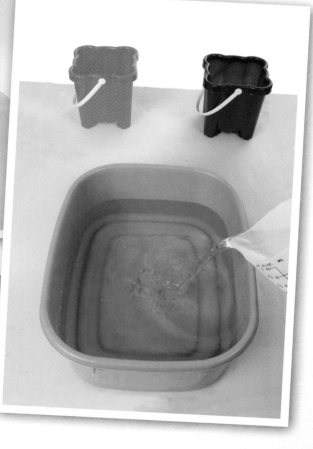

Step 1

Pour cold water and ice cubes into a bucket.

Step 2

Pour hot (not boiling) water into another bucket.

Step 3

Fill a large bowl with water at room temperature.

The hot water should be bearable to touch—don't burn yourself!

Step 4

Put one hand in the hot water and the other hand in the cold water. Your hands should stay in the water for a few minutes.

Step 5

Take your hands out, then plunge them both into the bowl of water at room temperature. The hot hand will feel cold, and the cold hand will feel hot!

Step 6

Take your hands out of the water and dry them.

How does it work?

This experiment proves that how we feel temperature is relative. If you have just been in a warm place, room temperature might feel quite cool, but if you have been in a cold place, room temperature will feel nice and warm.

215

Ice Cream in a Bag

Here is a simple way to make ice cream in just ten minutes—you'll never chase after the ice cream truck again!

You will need

- ½ cup (120 ml) whole milk or cream
- Sugar
- Vanilla extract
- 2 small ziplock freezer bags
- 1 large ziplock freezer bag
- 4 cups of ice cubes
- A rolling pin
- A clean dish towel
- Salt
- Woolen gloves

Step 1

Pour ½ cup (120 ml) whole milk or cream, 1 tablespoon of sugar, and ½ teaspoon of vanilla extract into a small ziplock freezer bag.

Step 2

Push out as much air as possible as you seal the bag.

Step 3

Place the first bag inside the second small bag, squeezing out the air.

Step 4

Seal the second bag.

Watch your fingers! And be careful with the table, too!

Step 5

Make some crushed ice. Fold the ice cubes in a clean towel and beat with a wooden rolling pin on a hard surface.

Step 6

Put the crushed ice in the large freezer bag, then add a tablespoon of salt.

217

Step 7

Put the smaller bags into the middle of the crushed ice and salt mixture in the large freezer bag. Squeeze out as much air as possible, and then seal the bag.

Step 8

Wearing the gloves, shake and squish the bag so that the ice surrounds the mixture. It should take 5 to 10 minutes for the mixture to become ice cream!

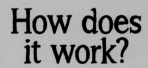

How does it work?

The salt lowers the freezing point of the ice. This means it melts faster. When it melts, it takes in energy in the form of heat from the surrounding environment—in this case, the ice cream mixture, which cools it down until it freezes.

Solar Oven

Harness the power of the sun to make tasty treats for you and your friends!

You will need

- An empty pizza box
- Black water-based paint
- A paint brush
- A thick black plastic bag
- Tin foil
- Plastic wrap
- A glue stick, tape, scissors, and a ruler
- A marker pen
- Marshmallows, chocolate, and cookies
- A paper plate
- A wooden stick
- A warm, sunny day!

Step 1

Paint the bottom and the sides of the outside of a pizza box black. Allow the paint to dry.

Step 2

Draw a 1 inch (2.5 cm) border on the front and sides of the top of the pizza box. Cut along the line with scissors.

Open the flap in the lid of the box. Stick a square of tin foil on the inside of the flap with the glue stick.

Step 4

Seal the opening made by the flap with a piece of plastic wrap.

Step 5

Line the inside of the pizza box with a folded black plastic bag. Tape it to the sides to keep it in place.

Step 6

Find a sunny spot in the yard. Close the window in the pizza box, and prop open the flap with a stick. Adjust the box so that the foil reflects the maximum sunlight through the window into the oven.

Step 7

Your oven is ready—let's make a tasty treat! Put a cookie on a paper plate and cover with marshmallows and chocolate.

Step 8

Check on progress in the oven every 10 minutes. Make sure sunlight is still reflected into the oven. On a nice, sunny day, it should take about 30 minutes.

How does it work?

The idea of a solar oven is to capture as much of the sun's heat as possible. The color black absorbs heat, so this makes sure that the cooking area of the box soaks up as much warmth as possible. Silver reflects heat, so the lid is used to gather more of the sun's heat and direct it to the food. The plastic wrap acts like glass in a greenhouse, allowing the light and heat in but not letting it out again. All three together make a pretty good oven!

Soap Sculptures

Create your own fun soap sculptures just using the microwave!

You will need

- 2 or 3 bars of luxury soap
- A microwave oven
- An oven glove
- Paper plates
- Plastic lids from aerosol cans

Step 1

Put a bar of soap on a paper plate. Ask an adult to put it in the microwave on a high setting for 1 minute.

WARNING!
Ask an adult to help you use the microwave.

Step 2

Watch through the closed door of the microwave. The soap should expand and grow!

Step 3

After one minute, the soap should have expanded, but if the original bar shape is still visible, microwave it for another 30 seconds.

Step 4

Allow several minutes for the soap to cool before you touch it. Remove it from the microwave with an oven glove.

Flatten the bottom of the sculpture so it sits on the stand.

Step 5

Repeat the process for each sculpture you want to make. Get your friends to make some—see who can get the best results! Make some stands from aerosol can tops to show off your work.

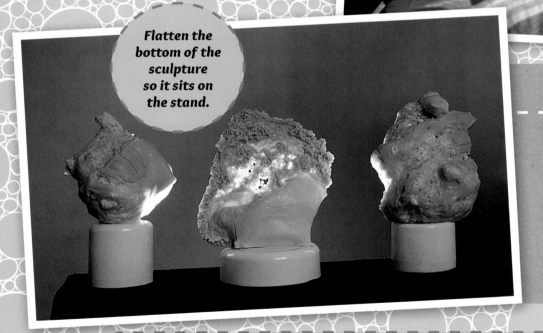

How does it work?

When the microwave is turned on, the water molecules in the soap are heated up and turn to vapor. The vapor forms bubbles that expand in the heat, making the soap expand in weird and wonderful ways!

223

Jumping Coin

Amaze your family and friends by making a coin jump into the air without touching it!

You will need

- A glass bottle with a narrow neck, such as a wine bottle
- A coin—the right size to fit on the mouth of the bottle
- Hot water
- Ice cubes
- 2 bowls—big enough for the bottle to stand in

Step 1

Put the empty bottle with the lid off in a bowl, then pack ice cubes around it. Allow it to cool for a few minutes. While you are waiting, ask an adult to pour some hot water into a bowl.

Step 2

Take the cold bottle out of the bowl. Put a coin on the mouth of the bottle.

Carefully lift the
bottle and put it in
the bowl
of hot water.

Step 4

After a little while,
the coin jumps off
the bottle!

How does it work?

As the bottle is heated, so is the
air inside it. As the air warms up,
it starts to expand, pushing on
the coin and making it jump.

Balloon Flame

You (and your adult helper) will need nerves of steel to test this fiery experiment!

You will need

- Balloons
- A candle on a saucer
- Matches
- Safety glasses or sunglasses
- Water

Step 1

Blow up a balloon and tie a knot in the end.

Step 2

Light a candle, then put on your safety glasses or sunglasses.

Step 3

Hold the balloon in the flame! What happens?

WARNING!

Be careful with the candle! Since the balloon may burst, do the experiment away from anything electrical or that may be damaged by getting slightly wet. Don't leave the balloon over the candle for more than ten seconds or so.

Step 4

Add some water to another balloon, then blow it up and knot it.

Step 5

Put the part of the balloon holding the water into the flame.

How does it work?

This is all about the conduction, or transfer, of heat energy. When the balloon is full of air, the candle flame melts the balloon's surface, so it explodes. That's because the heat remains concentrated over the candle. Water conducts heat better than air, so it can absorb some of the heat—keeping the balloon from melting.

Step 6

After a few seconds, remove the balloon from the flame and examine it!

Jar Wars

Insulators are materials that keep heat energy from spreading. They are used to keep things warm (or cold). This experiment hunts for the best insulators.

You will need

- 3 clean jars with lids, similar in size and shape
- A clean sock
- Bubble wrap
- An old newspaper
- Ice-cold water
- A clock, watch, or timer
- A cooking thermometer
- Tape
- Scissors

Step 1

Check that your jars are clean and that they have lids that fit well.

Step 2

Wrap each jar in a different material, with only one layer of material covering the sides of the jar.

228

Step 3

Secure the materials with tape, but don't cover the tops of the jars. Stand the jars in a row.

Step 4

Fill all the jars with ice-cold water.

Step 5

Record the temperature of the water in each jar. Put all the lids on the water-filled jars. Note the time.

How does it work?

If you can find a material that is not good at passing heat on, it will be a good insulator. If the heat from the air isn't passed on to the water, the water will remain cold for longer. Which material was the most effective insulator? Can you find another that is better?

Step 6

Wait five minutes—check the time. Take the temperature again in each jar. Compare the temperatures. Which jar kept the water coldest?

SUPER POWER

In this chapter, you'll find facts and experiments that explore the amazing science of electricity and magnetism.

An electric eel is an amazing creature with a pretty cool superpower. It is capable of generating powerful electric shocks, which it uses for hunting, self-defense, and communicating with other eels.

Making a Circuit

Electricity is carried in a circuit. A circuit is a kind of loop through which electricity flows. We are going to make our own circuit.

You will need

- Insulated wire
- MES bulb
- Bulb holder
- Tape
- AA battery
- Board
- Scissors
- Paper clips
- Thumbtacks

Circuit diagram

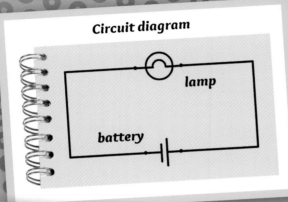

lamp

battery

Step 1

Use board to build your circuit on. This is a piece of soft board, but you could use wood or plywood. Make it about 12 x 8 inches (30 x 20 cm).

WARNING!
Ask an adult to help you.

Step 2

Prepare your wire by stripping the colored insulation from both ends. You can do this with a pair of scissors, but you'll need an adult to help.

Step 3

We've fixed the lamp to the board with some tape to make things tidier.

Step 4

Fix one end of each wire to the lamp and the other ends to the battery using tape.

How does it work?

The lamp comes on because we've made a continuous circuit connecting the battery and lamp. If the lamp doesn't come on right away, try turning the battery around.

Make a battery holder

Use two paper clips (not plastic coated) and two thumbtacks to make a battery holder like this.

The battery should be held firmly in place between the paper clips.

Alternatively, you can use a battery holder to give a reliable fixing point for the wires.

Go with the Flow

Which materials can electricity flow through? Those that allow electricity to pass through them are called conductors. Those that don't are called insulators. Use the circuit from page 233 to find out whether materials are conductors or insulators.

You will need

- The circuit from page 233
- Insulated wire
- Ballpoint pen
- Metal tape measure
- Nail
- Flower
- String
- Coin

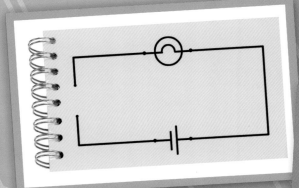

Step 1

Strip the insulation from the wire as you did on page 232. Add a new wire to the circuit we made on page 233.

Step 2

We are going to use the ends of the wires to test different materials.

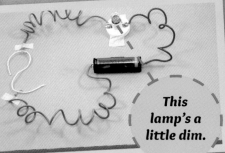

Step 3

A plastic pen doesn't complete the circuit. Neither does the string.

This lamp's a little dim.

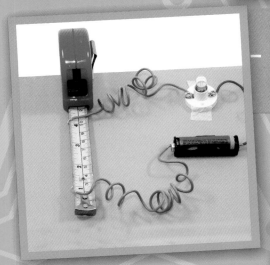

Step 4

The paint on the tape measure is resisting the current.

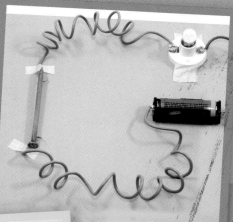

Step 5

This nail completes the circuit.

Step 6

So does tin foil.

Step 7

Will this coin complete the circuit? What about the flower?

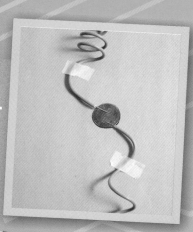

How does it work?

Most conductors are metal. We use insulators such as plastics to stop electricity from going where we don't want it to go.

Look at these tools. Why do you think they have thick, rubbery handles?

235

Turn It On!

We've made a circuit that lights lamps, but we probably don't want it to be on all the time. Let's make a simple switch to turn the lamp on and off.

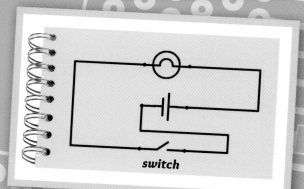

switch

Step 1

Your paper clip must be made of metal and not painted or coated with plastic.

Step 2

Test the paper clip as a conductor by the method we used in the last experiment.

Step 3

Bend the paper clip a little in the middle.

Step 4

Bend the bare wire end of one of the wires around a thumbtack, then press it into the soft board.

Step 5

The other thumbtack holds the other wire and the paper clip in place.

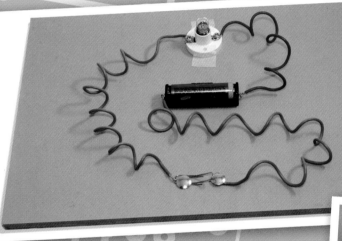

Step 6

Here's the switch in the circuit.

Step 7

Press the switch to turn the lamp on!

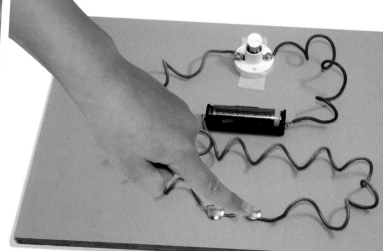

How does it work?

Electricity flows when there's no break in the circuit.

Bright Ideas

You will need

- The circuit from the last experiment
- 2 more bulbs and lamp holders
- 2 short pieces of wire with insulation stripped from the ends

What happens when we want more light? Do we make more circuits like the one on the last page, or can we just add more lamps to the circuit? Let's find out! We are going to connect more bulbs to the circuit.

Experiment 1

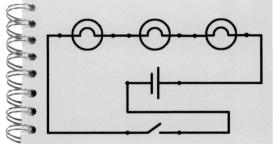

Step 1

Take the circuit we made on pages 236–237. Make sure the switch is turned off.

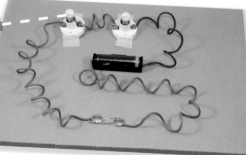

fairly dim

Step 2

Connect another lamp in the circuit next to the first one. Turn on the current.

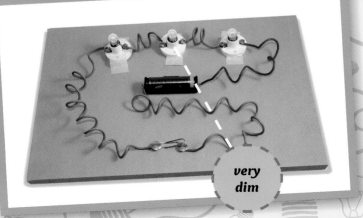

Step 3

Turn it off, and connect another lamp to the circuit to make three. Turn it on again.

very dim

How does it work?

We've connected the bulbs together in the circuit like a daisy chain. This is called a series circuit. Every bulb we add to the circuit increases the energy required for the electricity to flow.

Lamps in series

Experiment 2

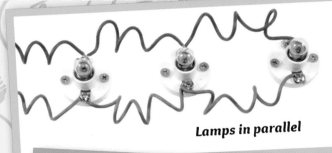

Lamps in parallel

There's another way to use electricity in a circuit, in parallel. Let's see what difference it makes to the result.

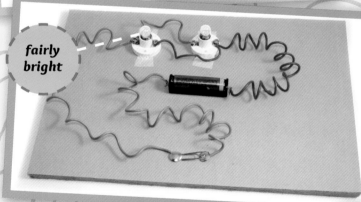

fairly bright

Step 1

Start as in Step 1, page 238. Connect one more lamp in the way shown above, using two more wires. Turn it on.

Step 2

Turn it off, then connect a third lamp with two more wires, as in the diagram above. Turn it on again.

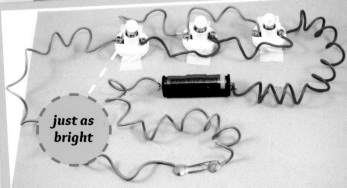

just as bright

How does it work?

This time, we've connected the lamps in parallel. Each bulb in the circuit gets the right amount of electricity to make it work. The battery might not last for long running three bulbs, though.

Lightning Strikes!

Lightning is a flash of electricity that is produced during a thunderstorm. All thunderstorms produce lightning and are very dangerous. Lightning is an electric current. Within a thundercloud way up in the sky, small pieces of ice (frozen raindrops) bump into each other as they move around in the air. All of those little collisions make an electric charge. After a while, the whole cloud fills up with electrical charges, and lightning lights up the sky.

The Lemon Battery

When you get tired of buying fresh batteries for your experiments, here's a way of making your own. The trouble is, you may have to buy some lemons instead! We are going to produce electricity and power a device using fresh fruit!

You will need

- 3 ice pop sticks
- Tin foil (this is really made of aluminum)
- 3 lemons
- 8 paper clips
- 3 pieces of copper tube about 4 inches long (10 cm)
- Insulated wire
- An old calculator with an LCD
- Small knife

WARNING!
Ask an adult to help you cut the holes in the lemons.

Step 1

Get an adult to cut a square hole and a slot in each lemon with a small knife.

Step 2

Wrap the ice pop sticks with tin foil, and push one into the slot of each lemon.

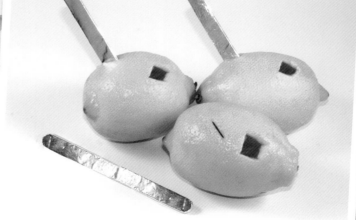

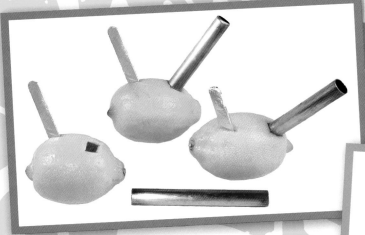

Step 3

Push one piece of copper tube into each lemon.

Step 4

Use paper clips to attach the wires.

Step 5

Ask an adult to open your calculator, remove the battery, and reveal the terminals. This calculator has a red wire marked "+" and a black wire marked "−."

WARNING!
Ask an adult to help you with steps 5 and 6.

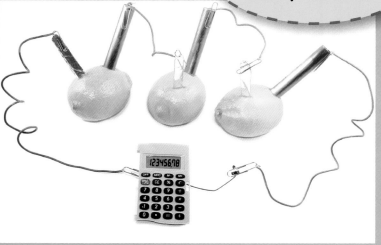

How does it work?

If we've made all the right connections, after a few minutes we should see the display come on. (If there's a switch, make sure it's on!) Our lemon battery is producing a charge by having two different metals (aluminum and copper) in an acid liquid (the juice of the lemon). A chemical reaction takes place, which also produces an electrical charge. The electricity is conducted through the lemon juice, into the metal, and on into the circuit.

Step 6

Connect the "+" wire to the foil and the "−" wire to copper. In between, make sure copper connects to aluminum (foil). Ask an adult to help.

This Page Is Alarmed!

Now that we know how to make a circuit with a battery, lamp, and switch, it's time to put our knowledge to good use! We are going to make a simple alarm system. It's operated by an intruder stepping on a special switch called a pressure mat.

Step 1

Stick foil to both sheets of card.

Step 2

Cut the sponge into strips about 1 inch (2.5 cm) wide.

Step 3

Stick the sponge strips on one foil-covered sheet with a glue stick.

Step 4

Put a paper clip on the edge of the foil. Attach a long wire to the paper clip.

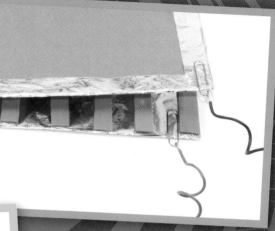

Step 5

Put a paper clip with a long wire on the other sheet.

Step 6

Use tape to join the two sheets together, foil side inward. Make sure the paper clips and bare wires can't touch accidentally. This is your new switch.

Bu u z z z z z z z z z z...

Step 7

Remove the paper clip from the circuit, and connect your two wires to the thumbtacks. Replace the lamp with a buzzer.

Step 8

Put the new switch under a mat and then stand on it.

How does it work?

The weight of someone standing on the pad will complete the circuit and set off the alarm.

Attractive Stuff

There's a close connection between electricity and another natural force—magnetism. Before we find out more about this, we need to look at magnets—what they are and how they are made.

You will need

- At least one magnet
- Some objects to test for magnetism, including some made of metal
- Nail
- Hammer
- Piece of wood

Experiment 1

Step 1

Take a magnet and hold it near various objects. Which objects are attracted to it?

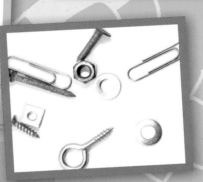

Step 2

The objects on the right are attracted to the magnet; those on the left are not.

Step 3

It seems that all the things that the magnet will pick up are metal. But not all metal things are magnetic. Try the magnet with some tin foil (aluminum).

How does it work?

All things that are magnetic contain iron. So, for instance, steel can be attracted by a magnet because steel is made of iron mixed with other elements.

Experiment 2

Step 1

Take a nail and stroke it lengthwise with one end of the magnet, lifting it away at the end, always using the same end of the magnet.

Step 2

The new magnet won't be as strong as the one that made it, but it can still pick things up!

WARNING!
Ask an adult to help you with the hammer.

Step 3

Put the magnetized nail on a firm surface, then tap it with a hammer along its length. Don't bend it!

Step 4

We have destroyed the magnetism in the nail.

How does it work?

Nails are made of iron in which the molecules are like little magnets arranged randomly. The effect of all the little magnets is to cancel out each other's magnetism. A magnet works because its molecules are all pointing the same way. Stroking a piece of iron (the nail) with a magnet gradually lines up the molecules, magnetizing it. Hitting the nail with a hammer jars the molecules back into their random arrangement, destroying the magnetic effect.

Magnetic Games

Let's look a little more closely at what magnetism can do. We are going to look at the ability of magnetism to pass through materials.

Experiment 1

Step 1

Copy the maze onto a sheet of cardstock, or draw your own. You and a friend will each need a magnet and paper clip.

You will need

- **Two magnets**
- **Marker pen**
- **Sheet of thin cardstock**
- **Two paper clips (different colors would be best)**
- **A glass jar with a plastic lid, clear sides, and no labels**
- **Colored pens**
- **Paper**
- **Scissors**
- **Tape**
- **A clean cookie sheet (check that a magnet will stick to it)**

Step 2

Starting at opposite ends, you each guide your paper clip through the maze using magnets under the cardstock. Each of you chooses an entrance and aims for the exit on the other side. When you're finished, try playing the game again—but this time with the card on a metal cookie sheet. Will the game still work?

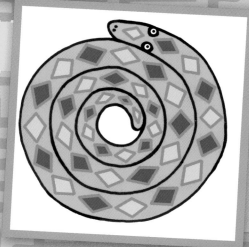

Experiment 2

Step 1

Copy the snake onto paper. Make it a little smaller if necessary, so that it fits in the bottom of the glass jar. Color it in, then cut out in a spiral shape. Put a paper clip on the snake's head.

Step 2

Tape the tip of the tail to the bottom of the jar.

Step 3

Secretly hold a magnet in the palm of your hand as you gently turn the jar upside down and back again.

Step 4

The snake stays up! Take your hand away (with the magnet), and the snake falls down.

How does it work?

In Experiment 1, magnetism passes through the card easily but not through metal. In Experiment 2, the snake trick reminds us that just because we can't see something (magnetism), it doesn't mean there's nothing there.

249

The Magnetic Earth

A magnet has a north pole and a south pole, and so does the Earth. What's the connection? We are going to experiment with some magnets and a simple compass.

You will need

- Bar magnet
- Piece of paper
- Small compass
- Pen or pencil

Step 1

Put a magnet on some paper. Draw around it so that you can replace it if it gets moved out of position.

Step 2

Move a compass around the magnet in small steps. Draw arrows in each position to show the direction of the compass needle.

Step 3

Continue drawing arrows all around the magnet.

Step 4

The arrows are beginning to form a pattern.

Step 5

Connect the little arrows to make curved lines.

How does it work?

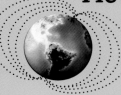

You've drawn a map of a magnetic field! The magnetic field around Earth is very similar.

Mighty Magnets!

People have known about magnets for thousands of years, and they've been using them practically, as compasses, for almost as long. The ancient Greeks and Romans knew that lodestone (an iron-rich mineral) could attract other pieces of iron. Today, magnets are used in industries all around the world in various forms.

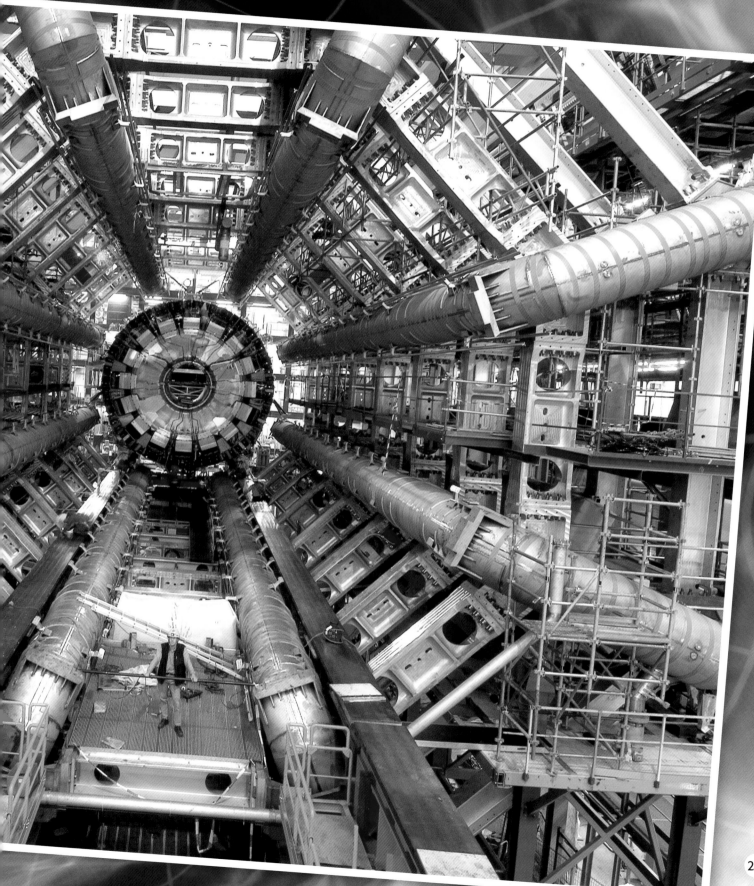

Glossary

Accelerate
Increase velocity.

Air pressure
The force of air as it pushes on things.

Air resistance
A type of friction that slows an object's movement through the air.

Alkali
Substance that forms a chemical salt when combined with an acid.

Alkaline
Describes a compound that contains an alkali.

Atom
Smallest particle that makes up a chemical element.

Bacteria
A large group of single cell microorganisms, some of which cause diseases.

Balance
Method used to compare the weights of objects.

Celsius
Scale of temperature measurement most commonly used in science.

Center of gravity
The point that marks the center of an object's mass, so that it acts as a balancing point.

Centrifugal force
The force that draws a rotating object away from the center of rotation.

Chlorophyll
Chemical that green plants use to help make their food.

Circuit
An electrical circuit is a closed loop, with electricity flowing around it.

Circumference
The distance around a circle.

Compass
An instrument for finding directions. It consists of a magnetized pointer that always points north.

Compost
Decayed organic material used as a fertilizer for growing plants.

Conduction
Heat moving from a hotter part of a solid to a cooler part.

Convection
The movement of heat through a liquid or gas caused by hot material rising.

Cycle
A series of events that repeat themselves in the same order.

Density
Degree of compactness of a substance.

Developing
Growing and becoming larger or more advanced.

Displace
To take the place of something.

DNA
A complicated chain of chemicals inside each cell, giving each organism its special qualities.

Echo
A sound caused by the reflection of sound waves from a surface back to the listener.

Enzyme
A chemical that speeds up the way in which substances react with each other.

Equilibrium
The balance between two or more objects or forces.

Evaporate
To turn from liquid into vapor.

Friction
A force that slows moving objects.

Fungi
Spore-producing organisms that feed on organic matter.

Hero's Engine
Invented by Hero of Alexandria in about AD 62, a heated tank that spins by shooting steam from one or more openings.

Identical
Exactly alike, the same as.

Illusion
An unreal image or impression, a false idea.

Inertia
The way matter continues in its existing state, unless changed by an external force.

Iron filings
Iron filings are very small pieces of iron that look like a dark powder. They are sometimes used in magnetism demonstrations to show a magnetic field.

Kinetic energy
The energy that a body possesses while it's moving.

LCD
Stands for liquid crystal display, a way of displaying shapes, numbers, or letters by applying a current to liquid crystals.

Lens
A piece of glass with one or both sides curved for concentrating or dispersing light rays.

Lift
Upward pressure on an aircraft wing caused by forward motion.

Magnet
A material or object that produces a magnetic field.

Magnetism
A way that a material attracts or repulses another material.

Margarine
Spread used instead of butter, made from vegetable oils and animal fats.

Mass
The amount of basic particles that an object has, which on Earth also indicates how heavy that object is.

MES
Stands for miniature Edison screw and relates to a light bulb fitting. It is named after Thomas Edison, the inventor.

Microorganism
A living creature that is too small for us to see with the naked eye.

Molecule
A group of atoms bonded together to form a chemical compound. A molecule is the smallest particle that still has all of the chemical properties of a substance.

Neutral
In chemistry, a neutral solution is neither acidic nor alkaline.

Nutrients
Substances that provide food needed for life and growth.

Observation
Statement about what you have learned by using your senses, e.g., heard or seen.

Periscope
A tube or box containing mirrors, designed to increase vision in submarines.

Pigment
A material that changes the color of light it reflects.

Pole
The end of a magnet, north or south, where its magnetic force is strongest.

Polymer
A chemical structure made up of repeating chains of molecules.

Potential energy
Energy in an object, such as heat in a hot water or tension in a stretched balloon.

Pressurized
Receiving a constant high force.

Propulsion
Action of driving or pushing forward.

Radiation
A form of energy traveling as rays or waves. Radiation can travel through a vacuum.

Sustained
Something that is kept going over time.

Smoke
Tiny particles, mostly carbon, distributed through the air.

Temperature
The degree or intensity of heat present in a substance.

Thriving
Doing well, developing correctly.

Transplant
To move to another place or situation or replant a plant.

Velocity
Speed of something in a particular direction.

Virtual
Not really existing as a solid object, appearing as an image or reflection.

Volume
Space occupied by a substance or object, or within a container.

Xylem
Plant cells that contain tubes to help the plant draw water and other materials upward.